Since 1888, *National Geographic* magazine has provided its readers a wealth of information and helped us understand the world in which we live. Insightful articles, supported by gorgeous photography and impeccable research, bring the mission of the National Geographic Society front and center: to inspire people to care about the planet. The *Explore* series delivers *National Geographic* to you in the same spirit. Each book highlights the work of National Geographic Explorers, photographers, and writers. Explore the world of *National Geographic*. You will be inspired.

ON THE COVER
Moche diadem, or
headpiece, A.D. 100–800

A SPECIAL NOTE ABOUT THIS BOOK

The inspiration for *Explore Peruvian Gold* was an exhibition of pre-Inca artifacts from Peru's royal tombs and other ancient splendors at the National Geographic Museum. These beautiful and unique objects—many of them gold—made a rare appearance outside of Peru in the spring of 2014. National Geographic Learning and the NG Museum collaborated to capture many of these objects and the stories behind them in this book.

MUSEO LARCO
LIMA-PERÚ

SPECIAL THANKS TO

EMBASSY OF PERU, AMBASSADOR HAROLD FORSYTH

MINISTRY OF CULTURE OF PERU

MUSEUM OF THE CENTRAL RESERVE BANK OF PERU

LARCO MUSEUM

**NATIONAL MUSEUM OF ARCHAEOLOGY,
ANTHROPOLOGY, AND HISTORY OF PERU**

SICAN NATIONAL MUSEUM

IRVING ARTS CENTER, IRVING, TEXAS

NATIONAL GEOGRAPHIC

Gary E. Knell	President & CEO
Terry D. Garcia	Chief Science and Exploration Officer
Gregory McGruder	Vice President, Public Programs
Fredrik Hiebert	Guest Curator, Archaeology Fellow

NATIONAL GEOGRAPHIC MUSEUM

Kathryn Keane	Vice President, Exhibitions
Richard M. McWalters	Director of Museum Operations
Abigail Bysshe	Traveling Exhibitions Manager
Ivan (Spanky) Campbell	Technical Coordinator
Brendan Cartwright	Visitor Services
Matt DeOrio	Exhibitions Coordinator
Rita Dooley	Special Events Manager
Cynthia Doumbia	International Traveling Exhibitions Specialist
Jennifer Fujii	Visitor Services
Elena Guarinello	Exhibition Development Manager
Brit Harner	Graphic Designer
Lauren Ippolito	Administration Coordinator
Lisa M. Kopp	Director of Visitor Services
Julia Louie	Exhibition Designer
Jordan McGirk	Visitor Services
Ivo Morales	Technical Coordinator
Thomas Oelberger	Exhibition Designer
Alan M. Parente	Art Director
Lauren Petruzzi	Budget Manager
Laura W. Ressler	Marketing Manager
Ellen Tozer	Retail Manager
Patrick Truby	Senior Graphic Designer
Catherine C. Tyson	Curator

The following individuals and National Geographic divisions assisted with the development, fabrication, and promotion of this exhibition: Agnes Tabah, Jane Terry, Joan Hewitt, Audiovisual, Carpenter Shop, Communications, Electronics Shop, General Services, Imaging, Magazine, Insurance and Risk Management, Law, Business, and Government Affairs, Maps, Paint Shop, Research, Conservation, and Exploration, and Visitor Services.

PERUVIAN GOLD

Kathryn Keane
Museum Director
Vice President, Exhibitions
National Geographic Museum

What is it about gold? For thousands of years, humans have admired it, treasured it, and shaped it into wondrous forms. For some, gold may symbolize eternity because it is unchanging. Gold never tarnishes, rusts, or loses its luster. Perhaps we love gold simply because it gleams so beautifully in the light.

The art of goldsmithing—creating artifacts and jewels from gold— has a long history. Some of the greatest goldsmiths may have been the peoples living in Peru before the Spanish arrived in the early 1500s. In the first centuries A.D., the Moche people were creating masks, statues, and jewelry from gold and other metals. The Moche were followed by the Wari, the Sicán, and the Inca. Each was a distinct culture that developed its own artistic vision in gold.

In 2014, the National Geographic Society hosted an exhibition that brings together gold artifacts from Peru's pre-Inca cultures. *Peruvian Gold: Ancient Treasures Unearthed* appeared at the National Geographic Museum in Washington, D.C. It showcased some of the most dazzling works from Peru's early history and opened a window into the early cultures of Peru. The exhibition also honored the century-long association between the National Geographic Society and Peru, which began in 1912 when the Society sponsored Hiram Bingham's expedition to Peru. On that voyage, he documented the stunning mountaintop ruins of Machu Picchu. Since that time, the Society has funded more than 180 scientific excavations in Peru.

In this book, you will find articles adapted from *National Geographic* magazine about the cultures featured in the *Peruvian Gold* exhibition. You'll find that the true value of Peruvian gold lies not in what it's worth but in the insights it brings into the people who came before us.

GOLDEN CUPS
These gold beakers, or cups, feature the face of the Sicán Deity and toads, which symbolized fertility.

NATIONAL
GEOGRAPHIC

CURATOR'S
JOURNAL

with **Fredrik Hiebert**

In 2014 the National Geographic
Museum hosted *Peruvian Gold:
Ancient Treasures Unearthed*,
an exhibition of artifacts from
pre-Inca Peru.

Here, curator Dr. Fredrik
Hiebert, National Geographic's
Archaeology Fellow, looks at
the artifacts with the practiced
eye of an archaeologist and
highlights the continuity of
cultures the objects reveal.
He also reflects on the very
special quality that gold
imparts—it's no wonder that
these objects catch our eye
and trigger our imaginations.

National Geographic Learning: Can you explain where these objects were found and how they were uncovered?

Fred Hiebert: All of these artifacts were found in Peru and belong to the national museum collections of Peru. Most of the museum quality objects actually came from non-scientific contexts; that is, we can't say exactly where they were originally found. However, archaeologists' careful excavations today provide that necessary context—what these types of objects meant to people in the past, how they were made, and how they were used.

NGL: What condition were these objects in when they were unearthed?

Fred Hiebert: Most of the objects were found buried, either in burials or in old, collapsed buildings. All the objects in the museums' collections have been carefully cleaned and restored to their original appearance. It is a slow and careful job, but it is very satisfying to finally see the artifacts as they originally were one or two thousand years ago.

NGL: What do we know about the tools and methods the artists might have used?

Fred Hiebert: The pre-Inca Peruvians were incredibly skilled craftspeople. All of the artifacts were made by hand. Metalworking, stone carving, pottery, and weaving were probably done in large workshops. There was no "market" where these were sold. All of them were produced for the religious and political leaders who used the objects in life and were buried with them. They were obviously very important things.

NGL: Which Peruvian cultures are represented in this exhibition?

Fred Hiebert: All of the artifacts in the exhibition belong to the pre-Inca cultures of Peru. The earliest are more than 3,500 years old. My favorites are artifacts from the earliest period of civilization in Peru: from 1000 B.C. Paracas (on the south coast); Cupisnique (from the north coast); and Chavín (from the highlands). They are all distinctive, but they share designs that allow us to understand the origins of Andean

civilization, which represents a region much larger than just Peru. That's pretty cool.

NGL: What can we learn from these artifacts about their cultures of origin?

Fred Hiebert: When we see the artifacts all together—from the earliest period of civilization through to the most elaborate—what we see is a continuity of their traditions, beliefs, and rituals. One of the most important lessons is seeing the continuity of these beliefs and rituals up until modern times, a fact that makes Peru and South America very special.

NGL: Your work takes you from the field to the preservation lab to the public museum. Which role do you prefer?

Fred Hiebert: Doing field archaeology— digging in and researching past settlements and structures—is only one side of the coin of archaeology. The other side is presenting these finds to the public and preserving them.

MOUNTAINS AND VALLEYS
Peru's pre-Columbian civilizations thrived in the mountains and valleys of the Andes. These agricultural terraces near Pisac show how they farmed on steep slopes.

Even though I am the National Geographic Archaeology Fellow and have presented my finds in print and on television, I most love having people visit the artifacts in person. An exhibition is like walking into the pages of *National Geographic* magazine. Seeing the artifacts in person is amazing.

NGL: Do you have a favorite story about a particular object from the exhibit?

Fred Hiebert: My favorite story is about a professor of archaeology when I was a graduate student. My teacher, Izumi Shimada, kept going into the field and disappearing for months at a time. Where was he? Little did I know that he was uncovering for the first time the richest and most important burial ever found in the Sicán valley of Peru (see page 48). He was so modest about his discovery that we students didn't know about the discovery until long after the final exam.

NGL: Can you explain the problem of the looting of cultural sites?

Fred Hiebert: Artifacts represent the history and record of people living in a region. When sites are robbed of their objects, not only is it illegal, but it makes people sad. People need to know that they can live without being robbed. The trade in artifacts is quite large, and it is part of an international network of dealers. Many governments today, including Peru, have made the digging and export of artifacts illegal. The United States and other countries are helping to enforce those rules.

NGL: What do you most want us to remember about Peru's pre-Inca cultures?

Fred Hiebert: The most important story is that pre-Inca Peru is just as important a center of civilization as ancient Egypt, ancient China, or ancient India. The richness of Peru's mountains, valleys, and coasts provided a hearth for these civilizations. Peru has contributed to our world by introducing new traditions, arts, and products that we use everyday around the world.

A WALK THROUGH THE EXHIBITION WITH CURATOR
FREDRIK HIEBERT

PHOTOGRAPHS BY KEN GARRETT

This exhibition, *Peruvian Gold: Ancient Treasures Unearthed,* was organized here at National Geographic to celebrate the relationship between Peru and National Geographic. National Geographic has been involved in archaeology in Peru since 1912 when we sponsored our first archaeologist, Hiram Bingham, to go to Peru to investigate Machu Picchu, an Inca site. These artifacts are pre-Inca, from 3,500 years ago right up to the time of the Inca, around A.D. 1400. The exhibition is organized around excavations

done in Peru by National Geographic-sponsored archaeologists and published in the pages of *National Geographic.*

After Hiram Bingham, our first big discovery was made in 1946 and published in the April 1947 issue of the magazine by William Duncan Strong and Clifford Evans. Using just regular film cameras, they took only about 30 or 40 pictures on the expedition. They documented a warrior found intact with 12 beautiful stirrup-shaped ceramics and a copper burial mask. It was world-changing

COPPER FUNERARY MASK

This is a copper mask from the Moche, dated A.D. 100 to 800. It is from the same time period as that burial discovered in 1946. Though they didn't take a picture of it, this is exactly the type of mask that Duncan Strong and Clifford Evans excavated. It's a Moche deity, *Ai Apaec*, or the Creator. This is one of the most beautiful objects that we have in the exhibition and in this book.

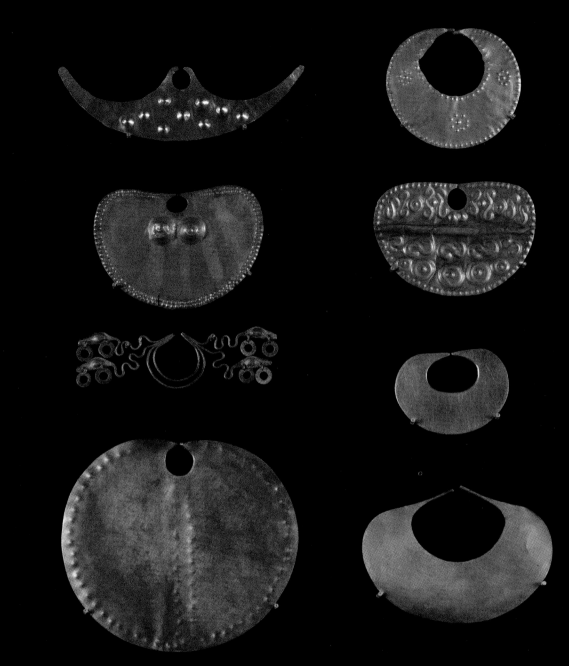

EAGLE POT AND NOSE ORNAMENTS

We're looking at a Moche portrait pot with an eagle headdress from about 2,000 years ago. This is a particularly important piece in the exhibition. Like the copper mask, it relates to the Strong and Evans article from 1947 because this pot is exactly like one in the photos from the 1947 *National Geographic* magazine article. I call these "Aha!" moments because we know that these objects are from museum collections, but we very rarely know about their original context.

And that's what is so special about having the *National Geographic* story behind all these artifacts. We know where they actually came from and what they would have looked like.

Nose ornaments like these from the Moche and Vicús cultures were used across Andean societies. They came in various shapes and sizes and were worn as decoration. Nose ornaments provided glitter and status to the ruler or the priest or the warrior who wore them.

FUNERARY ATTIRE

This spectacular piece is a headdress with a solid gold pectoral, or a breastplate, a huge necklace, and gigantic ear spools. I mean really, absurdly gigantic. It was crafted by the Chimú between A.D. 900 and 1470. But like so many of the museum-quality pieces in Peru, it was not excavated by archaeologists. There is a lot of mystery about this. What does it mean? Where did it come from, exactly?

It was most likely worn by a person of elite status buried at Chan Chan, the Chimú capital. The ear spools feature the Chimú lord, and the gold plumes on the crown symbolize birds and the sun. The epaulettes, or shoulder pieces, show the Chimú lord holding trophy heads. You might detect different colors of gold in these pieces because some are made of solid gold and others are made with alloys.

FINE-LINE STIRRUP VESSEL

The pre-Inca Peruvians were master craftspeople of textiles, metals, and ceramics. One example is this Moche stirrup vessel, a type of pot with two handles that come together in a single spout that pours in both directions. One of the things that makes these vessels mysterious is that there was no writing system that we know of for this culture. But when we study this vessel's fine-line paintings, we can see a story: figures wearing headdresses and running from the bottom, around the pot to the top, and back down again. It's not a single scene, but more like a comic strip.

I especially like the top of the vessel. It shows lima beans, which are seeds to be planted but which are also interpreted as symbols of fertility. Lima beans were sometimes painted and may have been used for counting or calendars. Someday we'll be able to read this pot like a book. We can't do it right now, but someday.

GOLD BEES

Now we're looking at a series of insects that were cut out of plate gold. These artifacts are from a special area of southern Peru called the Nasca. The Nasca area is most famous for these giant glyphs, huge drawings that were created in the desert and first discovered when people flew airplanes over them in the 1920s and 1930s. People who discovered the drawings couldn't believe that these patterns on the ground could have been made by people because you couldn't really see them except by airplane. All sorts of crazy myths emerged about the glyphs, including one about how aliens must have made them. But the fact is that when you actually do the archaeology, when you actually look at the people and the cultures of this area, you see those same designs.

Here in the exhibition we have a series of beautiful golden appliqués in the shape of insects or bees that would have been sewn onto clothing. This insect is exactly like one of the designs of these giant glyphs that were drawn on the pavement of the desert. This artifact helps us understand that the Nasca were the people who made those glyphs. You don't need to have aliens to come make them.

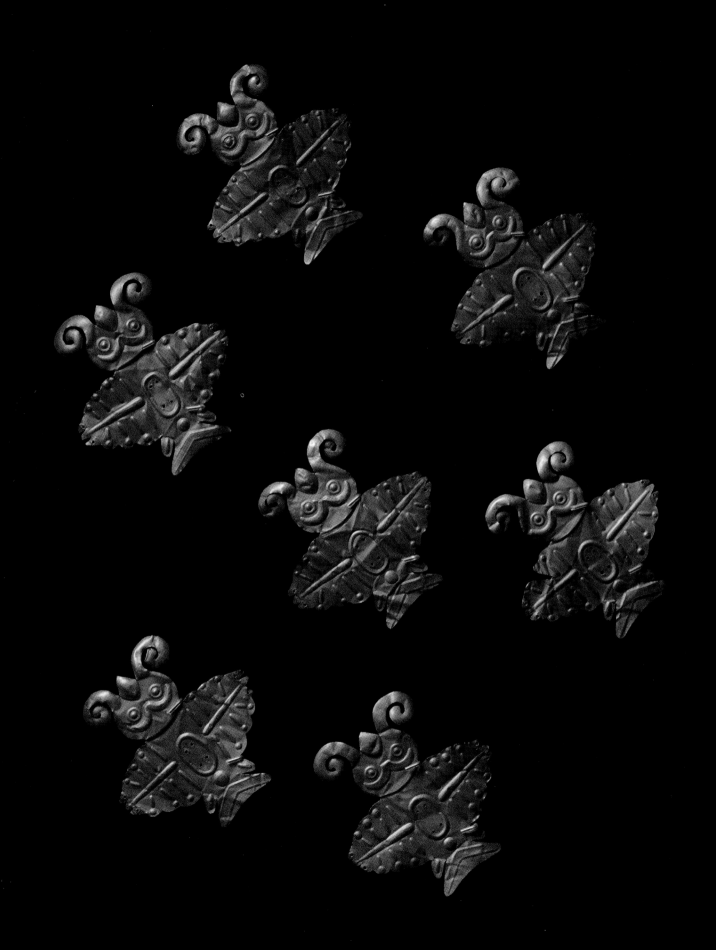

GOLD NECKLACES AND BRACELETS

Gold is a very special material around the world for its natural properties. The first thing about gold is that it's very soft. Anybody who has some gold knows that it's a soft metal that scratches easily. It's also very easy to work. If you don't have very sophisticated tools or a giant workshop, it still is possible to work gold.

The second thing about gold is that it gleams. It is such a beautiful metal. It gleams like the sun. In so many places around the world,

independently, cultures have decided there is a relationship between the gleam of gold and the gleam of the sun.

The third thing about gold is that it never rusts and it never tarnishes. It is the original eternal material so if you're trying to make a correlation between the afterlife and eternity, gold is the perfect material. This is true in Egypt, Mesopotamia, Europe, and of course in the New World, like Peru.

CATS AND SNAKES

Many common motifs, or themes, appear in the art of pre-Inca Peru. Two of those motifs are cats and snakes. Cats represented strength and fierceness; snakes symbolized the underworld and the fertility of the earth.

This textile (above left) is one of the earliest pieces of beautiful weaving in Peru. It is about 3,000 years old. It was used in a high status burial. Notice the interlocking figures of cats holding trophy heads and knives.

These two gold cut outs, a cat (far left) and a snake (left), are some of the earliest examples of goldsmithing in the whole area of the Andes; they are about 3,500 years old. These ornaments represent one of the first ways that people were using gold: to decorate clothing.

GOLD AND SILVER

Several hundred years later, more cats appear on this four-inch nose ornament (above) from the Vicús culture, which dates from 200 b.c. to a.d. 700. It is a bimetal, or two-metal, piece. On one side it is gold and on the other side, silver. What's important about this is that in pre-Inca Peru, gold was not used as a commodity. It was never turned into coins, and it was never traded. It was always symbolic.

On this nose ornament, the gold is the sun and the silver is the moon. They are two halves of a whole. That's their whole concept of the universe. The sky is above and the earth is underneath. Many, many artifacts from pre-Inca Peru demonstrate this dual symbolism: sun and moon, earth and sky, and other dual themes, such as life and death.

DIADEM

This artifact is featured on the cover of this book. It's a diadem, or a headpiece that symbolizes power and authority. It is 2,000 years old, and it's from the Moche culture. I particularly love this piece. About 12 inches wide, the diadem is made in this beautiful circular design cut from a single sheet of copper and silver coated with gold.

We have here an incredibly lively scene of a warrior. It's a person's head with a short, little stubby body as if the person is jumping up and down. The warrior is wearing a big headdress and holding two supernatural animals—part lizard, part cat—one on each side.

In 1988, on the pages of *National Geographic*, we helped sponsor the excavation of the largest intact Moche burial ever, Walter Alva's Lord of Sipán. In those excavations they found a headpiece very similar to this one. It's those kinds of archaeological stories, Walter Alva's research at Sipán or Strong and Evans' work, that help give context for these objects.

DRINKING VESSEL

Here we have a drinking vessel made by the Recuay culture in about A.D. 300. I just love this pot because it shows an actual, living activity of a drinking festival. The central figure is wearing ornamental garb, probably a gold mask with cinnabar, or red paint, on it. Notice the giant ear spools and animal-motif headdress on top. You can imagine that this ceremonial dress would look pretty daunting.

This vessel is also is a whistling pot, which means it whistles when you pour the liquid out. A Peruvian legend says these vessels were created specifically along the dry coast because people were very protective of their liquids there. If someone came to take your liquid, it would whistle and you would know that someone was taking it. It was a built-in alarm system. Whether that's true or not, it's a great story.

NATIONAL GEOGRAPHIC PHOTOGRAPHER **KEN GARRETT**

HOMETOWN: **GREAT FALLS, VIRGINIA**
CURRENT RESIDENCE: **BROAD RUN, VIRGINIA**
FIRST ASSIGNMENT FOR *NATIONAL GEOGRAPHIC*
"SQUARE-RIGGER: VOYAGE FROM BALTIC TO BICENTENNIAL," 1976

National Geographic photographer Ken Garrett gets up-close and personal with his subjects: Otzi the Iceman, King Tut, Mesoamerican gods, and a few Andean mummies, to name just a few. He and Fred Hiebert have worked together on many National Geographic assignments, including the photographs of the artifacts in this article. Both Garrett and Hiebert share a passion for preserving archaeological and historical treasures and helping people learn about them.

Garrett was first "featured" in *National Geographic* in 1957, when he was just three years old. The first photo he sold to the Society was taken off a television screen in 1969, the moment Neil Armstrong stepped off the lunar lander onto the moon. A few years later, after earning his B.A. in anthropology from the University of Virginia, Garrett dove right into photographic work with *National Geographic* magazine. Since his start, he has shot more than 50 stories for the magazine and has published several books.

During his distinguished, 30-plus year career with *National Geographic* magazine, he has specialized in capturing images of past civilizations, especially ancient Egyptian and Mesoamerican artifacts and ruins. Garrett's keen eye, subtle use of light and position, and fundamental appreciation and understanding of his subjects enlightens us all.

Discovering the New World's

RICHEST UNLOOTED TOMB

Adapted from "Discovering the New World's Richest Unlooted Tomb,"
by Walter Alva, in *National Geographic*, October 1988

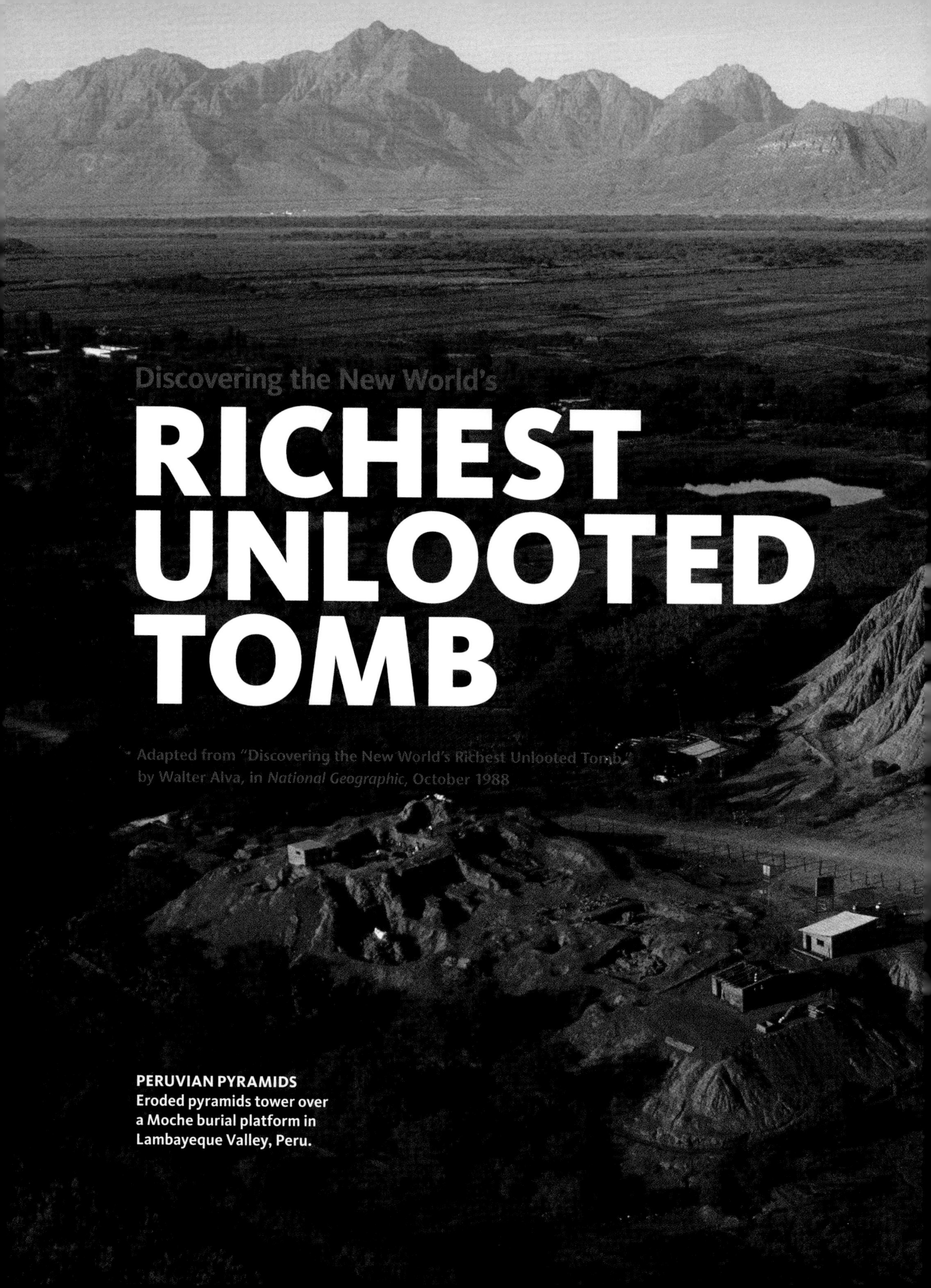

PERUVIAN PYRAMIDS
Eroded pyramids tower over
a Moche burial platform in
Lambayeque Valley, Peru.

Walter Alva is a Peruvian archaeologist famous for his excavations of the ruins of the Moche people, a civilization that flourished on Peru's northern coast 1,200 years before the Inca. In 1987, he made a spectacular discovery that yielded precious information about the mysterious Moche. One year later, fresh from the field, he wrote this account of his find.

A CALL IN THE NIGHT

The chief of police rang me near midnight. His voice was urgent: "We have something you must see—right now." Hurrying from where I live and work—the Brüning Archaeological Museum in Lambayeque, Peru—I wondered which of the early pyramids and ceremonial platforms had been robbed of its treasure this time.

These structures were built by the Moche. From about A.D. 100 to 700 these agricultural people lived in the desert between the Andes Mountains and the Pacific Ocean, building huge adobe monuments and laying within them their noblest dead. They also buried fine gold and pottery, which explains why Moche burials are rarely found untouched. The artifacts are taken and sold by middlemen to demanding Peruvian and foreign collectors on a **black market** for stolen pre-Columbian treasures.

The objects recovered from the house of a local **looter** were very impressive. They included the copper faces of two beautiful jaguar-like creatures. Just as remarkable were two gold peanuts, three times their natural size, wrinkled and ridged like the real thing.

Peru's grave looters' tradition is an old one. The first came in 1532, when Spanish conquistadores ransacked the Inca Empire for gold, silver, and gems. The Moche platforms and pyramids were also pillaged by the conquerors, and have been looted ever since by poor Peruvians for extra money. Peruvians today call these adobe structures *huacas* (HWAH-cahs), and the looters *huaqueros* (HWAH-kair-ohs).

MOCHE FELINES
These jaguar-like copper masks are covered in a thin layer of gold and have fangs made of shell.

The 33-foot-high ceremonial platform near the pyramid of Sipán presented an easy target for *huaqueros*. I can imagine them scurrying that night when by chance they penetrated a burial chamber within the platform. Posting armed lookouts, they worked quickly. The stakes were high. Police report that a little gold head identical to one they seized is now going for $60,000 on the black market.

Local police tried to recover the plunder. Several days after the raid on the platform they searched a looter's house. He was away, but behind the house they found dozens of telltale fragments of gilded, or gold-covered, copper.

PROTECTING TREASURE
Guards keep watch over the tomb
of a warrior-priest to ensure
artifacts are safe from looters.

The police mounted a second raid. This time there was a shootout, and one of the looters was fatally wounded.

The village was in shock. But the artifacts taken from the platform would lead to a magnificent discovery.

MOCHE INSIGHTS

The treasures unearthed by the looters could only have come from a tomb of unprecedented magnificence. Could the Moche of Peru, who built the massive platform 17 centuries ago, have hidden other royal tombs in its depths?

I believed so.

Now, a year of intensive excavation has revealed a second chamber. In it lies one of the richest tombs ever found in the Americas—the grave of an awe-inspiring leader, perhaps a warrior-priest. Because it is intact, it gives us the clearest picture we have of the Moche and the way they lived.

From this extraordinary burial we have recorded treasure after treasure. We have also found additional skeletons. This suggests that others were sacrificed and buried with the tomb's chief occupant, whom I have titled Lord of Sipán.

The treasures found show that the refined art and technology of the Moche rivaled that of the Maya. Their ceramics and weaving compare favorably with Peru's better-known Inca. The Moche also diverted rivers into canals, turning the desert into irrigated farmland that sustained well over 50,000 people.

But for all of their sophistication, the Moche never developed a writing system. Fortunately, the Moche decorated their pottery with scenes depicting their lives and rituals, which is where we get most of our information about them.

We were in a race to find the tomb before the nearby gold-crazed villagers. Using shovels and bare hands, they combed the platform for

LARGER THAN LIFE
This realistic gold peanut was fashioned to be part of one of two necklaces that were found on the warrior-priest.

anything the *huaqueros* might have missed. To gain control of the site, the police made surprise patrols. Meanwhile, we set up a tent at the site. Our immediate goal was modest: to rescue whatever had escaped the looters' pillage.

Tension ran high at first. Angry villagers viewed my team as nothing more than a higher class of thieves. Brothers of the slain *huaquero* shouted death threats. Several times we were shocked from sleep by bursts from the policeman's submachine gun—warnings to the *huaqueros* sneaking up in the dark.

Near the bottom of the 23-foot pit the looters had previously dug, we uncovered the first hint of what was to come. Here we found the imprints of wooden beams that had once roofed a small chamber. It was not part of the original construction, suggesting it was a burial chamber built after an important person died.

A possible insight into Moche ceremonial life emerged one day from the looted site. We found a heavy copper scepter, often carried by someone powerful, that the *huaqueros* had missed. It had a scene carved in miniature at the top. A supernatural creature, half cat, half reptile, was pictured performing a religious ritual.

From this we concluded that Sipán must have been an important spiritual center. The creature of the scepter appears on Moche pottery from widely separated locations, indicating his universal importance.

DIGGING TO THE PRIZE

As we finished clearing the looters' pit, we wondered whether the platform at Sipán concealed any other important Moche burials. As we probed farther, the imprint of another set of wooden beams suggested it might. The timbers had enclosed a rectangular chamber about four feet deep where sand had seeped in, filling the chamber below. Slowly we removed the sand with dustpans and paintbrushes.

At last the flick of a brush exposed the lid of a red clay pot. Now every stroke exposed other pots, bowls, beakers, and jars. We eventually inventoried over a thousand pieces, perhaps the greatest cache of pre-Columbian ceramics ever excavated.

Much of the found pottery was **utilitarian**. The Moche produced huge amounts of pottery for cooking and for storing water, dried beans, and corn. But other vessels were intricately decorated with scenes of warriors, women giving birth, and prisoners in restraints.

We next turned our attention to a different section of the platform. Our hopes soared when, 12 feet below the surface, we discovered a man's skeleton stretched out on his back. A fragmented helmet of gilded copper and a round copper shield covering his ribs indicated he had been a warrior. As we dug on, we began referring to this warrior as the "guardian." But, we wondered, who was he guarding?

We removed the guardian's delicate bones and began to probe for the boundaries of his burial chamber. We found the corner of a 15-foot square opening. Twenty inches below the guardian's level we again found traces of support beams.

Marks left by the beams in the earth and a few fragments of wood were revealing. Radiocarbon tests later dated them to about A.D. 290.

By now we knew that finding wood usually meant there was something interesting below. Soon our brushes uncovered a bright green bundle of copper strapping. We quickly dusted off seven more of the mysterious copper straps. Together they marked the boundary of a rectangle four feet wide and seven feet long. For long seconds words would not come. When we finally spoke, it was to babble: "A coffin! It's sealed. . . . Never opened!"

Now more than ever we worked as carefully as surgeons. Using artists' brushes and air squeeze bulbs we removed the dust and sediment, puff by puff. Each layer and object was carefully sketched and photographed in place. We could see that the contents of the coffin were jumbled, disturbed by the fall of the chamber roof.

From fragments of gilded copper backed with fabric we made out two weavings. One of them depicted four small figures of a man. The other showed the same man with arms raised and fists clenched. A V-shaped headdress of gilded copper two feet across bore another image of this man.

Lifting a small clod beside the copper sheeting we found a greater prize—a meticulously detailed thumb-sized man of hammered sheet gold, clad

INTRICATE BEADING
Colored shells and copper beads form this pectoral that would cover the chest.

in a turquoise tunic. This may be the finest single item of pre-Columbian jewelry ever found. Only under a microscope can the artist's workmanship be appreciated.

The figure grips a tiny war club in his right hand. A gold ornament hangs from his nose. He wears a necklace of pinhead-sized beads shaped like owl heads. Crescent-shaped bells hang from his belt. Only after reassembling the bits of gold and turquoise that surrounded him could we see that he had been the centerpiece of an ear ornament. On either side, a tiny warrior guarded him.

THE TOMB OF THE LORD OF SIPÁN

Now we began uncovering the skeleton and lavish grave goods of the man depicted in the thumb-sized figure: the Lord of Sipán. Among the treasures we found a pair of gold eyes, a gold nose, and a gold chin-and-cheek visor that had been placed on the Lord of Sipán's skull like a mask. Sixteen large gold disks had adorned his chest. The copper sandals on his feet were strictly ceremonial—they were too stiff to walk in.

There was much more. We found four headdresses—two large gold crescents and two cone-shaped caps adorned with copper.

Hundreds of tiny gold and turquoise beads formed elegant bracelets, and thousands of shell beads formed coverings for the chest, shoulders, and legs of the Lord of Sipán.

We found emblems of war: a small symbolic war club and a long rattle with a gold chamber resembling an inverted pyramid. Its copper handle was carved with shields and battle clubs and featured a wicked-looking blade. Holding the rattle gave me the uncomfortable feeling that the Lord of Sipán had known all too well how to use it.

And what of him, that fierce nobleman: How did he die? Was he young? Or old? His bones gave us some answers.

The skeleton of the Lord of Sipán was largely blackened splinters. We gathered pieces of his skull, but few other bones were found whole. Later examination of the remains showed the Lord of Sipán to be five and a half feet tall and in his early 30s when he died.

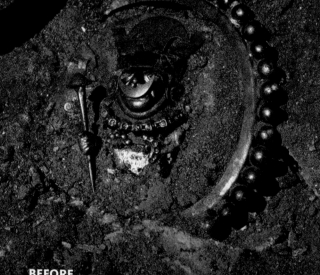

BEFORE
Shown as it was originally found in the warrior-priest's tomb, this miniature man of gold holds a war club and has a moveable nose piece.

AFTER
Considered to be perhaps the finest example of pre-Columbian jewelry ever found, this ear ornament is now cleaned and ready for display.

Mysteries of the Moche still baffled me,
but no matter — I had seen their majesty.

A QUESTION OF BALANCE

So what could have killed this young, apparently healthy man? Did he die suddenly, perhaps in an epidemic? Suddenly or not, the Lord of Sipán departed his people prematurely. A shocked and saddened society may have briefly teetered, losing its balance.

And balance, we have learned, was important to the Moche. I was reminded of this as I lifted a pair of necklaces from the Lord of Sipán's skeleton. Identical strings each held ten metal peanuts, similar to those looted. Five peanuts in each necklace were gold, and lay upon the Lord of Sipán's right side. Matching silver peanuts lay to the left. Similarly, a solid piece of gold was nestled amid the bones of his right hand and a solid piece of copper in his left. He lay with head to the south and feet to the north while his skeleton lay across the east-west axis of the platform. All Andean cultures—not just the Moche—pay close attention to the four cardinal points of the compass, which they refer to as the four quarters of the world.

At the head of the Lord of Sipán's coffin we uncovered the bones of a young woman. Predictably, at his feet we found the bones of another. Both women were about 20 when they died. One rested on her right side, head pointing west. Her opposite was exactly that, lying with her head to the east.

Head to head with the women and flanking the coffin lay the skeletons of two men. Copper shield, headdress, and war club marked one as a warrior. The other lay buried with a dog, perhaps the Lord of Sipán's prized hunting hound.

One evening, gazing in dreamy wonder, I watched the sun set behind the monuments at Sipán. I imagined a funeral procession making its way along a causeway across irrigated fields. Stricken Moche people watched as a **litter** carried the Lord of Sipán to his tomb. Following the litter came two young women escorted by a pair of warriors. One, the guardian, was joined by another man, hunting dog at his side. I pictured all their faces ecstatic, welcoming death.

As the sun's last rays faded and the Lord of Sipán's platform and pyramid melted into the shadows, I was thoughtful. Mysteries of the Moche still baffled me, but no matter—I had seen their majesty.

THINK ABOUT IT! ||||||||||||||||||||||||||||

1 **Sequence Events** What are the main events in the excavation of the tomb of the Lord of Sipán?

2 **Synthesize** While there are still mysteries surrounding the Moche, what did archaeologists learn about the culture from the excavation of the site at Sipán?

3 **Make Inferences** Why do you think the people buried with the Lord of Sipán might have welcomed death?

BACKGROUND & VOCABULARY

black market *n.* a system for buying and selling stolen or illegal goods

litter *n.* (LIH-tur) a covered seat for carrying one person

looter *n.* (LOO-tur) a person who robs or steals, especially on a large scale

utilitarian *adj.* (yoo-TIH-lih-TEH-ree-uhn) made to be useful rather than decorative

Unraveling the Mystery of the
Warrior-Priest

Adapted from "Unraveling the Mystery of the Warrior-Priest," by Christopher B. Donnan, in *National Geographic*, October 1988

MUSEO LARCO
LIMA-PERÚ

As the Sipán tomb was being excavated, everyone kept asking the same question: "Who was this person?"

Analysis of the bones indicated an adult male about 35 years old. The elaborate tomb, with its valuable grave goods, suggested a man of high status. But what was his role in society? Careful study of Moche art helps answer that question.

The Moche had no writing system, but they left a vivid artistic record. Many of their ceramic vessels were decorated with fine-line drawings of their buildings, tools, gods, and ceremonies.

The University of California, Los Angeles (UCLA) has collected more than 125,000 photographs of Moche art. The art provides clues about the man buried in the tomb at Sipán.

As the tomb was being excavated, photographs of the objects were sent to UCLA. They were compared to drawings on Moche ceramics, which showed how the tomb objects were worn, and which objects were worn together.

If the objects found in the coffin were worn and used by the man during his lifetime, it is almost certain that he was a warrior. Among them is a pair of gold-and-turquoise ear ornaments with standing figures. The central figure is a warrior holding a Moche war club and wearing a crescent-shaped headdress and a nose ornament. These items strongly suggest they were part of a warrior's costume. So were the two large backflaps found in the tomb. These are worn exclusively by warriors in Moche art.

Analysis of Moche art is key to uncovering the true identity of the man buried in the Western Hemisphere's richest unlooted tomb.

The fine craftsmanship of the tomb's combat objects, and the fact that they are made of gold and silver, are important clues. They indicate that this warrior was of high status and possessed special qualities. To understand why, we need to look at the role of warriors in Moche society.

Military scenes are common in Moche art. Many show warriors engaged in combat. A main purpose of Moche warfare was to capture enemy warriors. Once taken prisoner, their weapons and clothing were hung from the war clubs of their captors. After they were presented to the court, they were sacrificed.

The killing of captured warriors occurred at a special ceremony, a favorite subject of Moche artists. The ceremony involved certain participants, recognizable by their poses and garments.

One Moche ceramic bottle bears a detailed scene of the sacrifice ceremony. The illustration shown here is a reconstruction of the artwork on the bottle. In the lower center and lower right parts of this scene are ❶ *two captured warriors* sitting cross-legged, with their hands tied. In the upper left part, a ❷ *warrior-priest* receives a tall goblet from a ❸ *bird warrior*.

The warrior-priest, with rays emanating from his head and shoulders, is the primary figure. He is usually pictured with a ❹ *spotted dog*, and wears a cone-shaped helmet, crescent-shaped headdress, and warrior backflap. These items were found in the tomb. Was the man actually the warrior-priest we see in the ceremony?

Other evidence supports this conclusion. Beneath the warrior-priest in the scene is his ❺ *litter*, with rays projecting from the backrest. This was a seat used to carry the warrior-priest. A ❻ *rattle* like the one found in the tomb is shown above the front of the litter, with its handle on the right. Such rattles were used at sacrifice ceremonies. In the scene, the rattle clearly belongs to the warrior-priest. Since the man in the tomb was buried holding one, his identification as a warrior-priest seems certain.

The royal tomb that was looted at Sipán contained many objects similar to those found in the excavated tomb. These include large beaded bracelets, a crescent-shaped headdress ornament, and gold and silver peanut beads. And more significantly, there is a rattle much like the one in the excavated tomb.

These artifacts suggest that the looted tomb also contained a noble who acted as warrior-priest at sacrifice ceremonies. Was Sipán the burial place for warrior-priests? As more tombs are excavated, we may learn the answer.

The royal tombs at Sipán provide a rare chance to match excavated artifacts with those shown in Moche art. Maybe the greatest treasure the tombs provide will be clues that help unlock more mysteries of the Moche culture.

THINK ABOUT IT! |||||||||||||||||||||||||||||||||

Summarize Describe the method the author uses to try to determine the identity of the body found in the tomb.

35

Untouched

Adapted from "Untouched," by Heather Pringle, in *National Geographic*, June 2014
Photographs by Robert Clark

HANGING ON
Remarkably preserved, the hand of an Andean
noble still clutches a bit of burial cloth.

For decades, grave robbers plundered the Peruvian burial site called El Castillo de Huarmey. But they missed one royal tomb, hidden for more than 1,000 years. A team of archaeologists is now exploring the site, slowly revealing the story of the Wari in this remote part of Peru.

DISCOVERY AT EL CASTILLO

It is late afternoon along the Peruvian coast. Local workmen gather as archaeologists Miłosz Giersz and Roberto Pimentel Nita open a row of sealed chambers near the entrance of a tomb. Concealed under a layer of heavy brick, the small chambers hold large ceramic jars. Some bear the images of painted lizards. Others display grinning human faces. As Giersz pries open the final chamber, he grimaces. "It smells awful down here," he splutters. He peers into a large pot. It's full of decayed flies once drawn to the pot's contents, possibly human blood. The archaeologist backs away and stands up, slapping a cloud of dust from his pants. In three years of digging at this site, Giersz has encountered death everywhere. He's found traces of insects and the remains of snakes that died in the bottoms of pots. Africanized killer bees have swarmed out of the chambers and attacked workers.

Plenty of people had warned Giersz that exploring El Castillo would be difficult, and a waste of time and money. For at least a century looters had dug into the slopes of the massive hill. They were searching for tombs containing skeletons decked out in gold and wrapped in fine woven cloth. The serpent-shaped hill was pitted with holes, littered with very old human bones, and strewn with modern garbage and rags. Afraid of bringing sickness to their families, the looters had often tossed away their clothing before they returned home.

Giersz was determined to dig there anyway. Something important had happened at El Castillo 1,200 years ago. Giersz was sure of that. Bits of cloth and broken pottery from Peru's little-known Wari civilization dotted the hill. Using an instrument that measures differences in Earth's magnetic field, Giersz and a small research team began imaging what lay underground. They also began taking aerial photos with a camera on a kite. The results revealed something that the grave robbers had missed: the faint outlines of buried walls. Giersz and a Polish-Peruvian team applied for permission to begin digging.

The outlines turned out to be a maze of towers and high walls spread over the entire southern end of El Castillo. Once painted dark red, the complex seemed to be a Wari temple dedicated to ancestor worship. In the fall of 2012, as the team dug down beneath a layer of heavy bricks, they made an amazing discovery: an unlooted royal tomb. Inside were four Wari queens or princesses and at least 54 other noble individuals. Buried with them were more than a thousand Wari goods. These included huge gold ear ornaments, silver bowls, and copper axes. All were of the finest workmanship.

"This is one of the most important discoveries in recent years," says Cecilia Pardo Grau, an expert in pre-Columbian art. As Giersz and his team continue to explore the site, analysis of their finds is shedding new light on the Wari and their wealthy ruling class.

WARI LORDS
Painted pots depicting Wari lords are among the treasures from the unlooted tomb at El Castillo de Huarmey.

THE WARI EMPIRE

The Wari rose to glory in the seventh century A.D., long before the rise of the powerful Inca. They became master engineers, building **aqueducts** and canals to supply water to their terraced fields. Near the modern Peruvian city of Ayacucho, they founded their capital, known today as Huari. At its peak Huari had a population of as many as 40,000 people. In contrast, Paris at the time had no more than 20,000 inhabitants. From this stronghold the Wari lords expanded their rule hundreds of miles along the Andes and into the coastal deserts. Many archaeologists consider theirs the first empire in Andean South America.

Researchers have long puzzled over how the Wari built and ruled this vast empire. Was it through conquest or persuasion or some combination of both? Unlike most great powers the Wari had no system of writing and left no recorded narrative history. But the rich finds at El Castillo, some 500 miles northwest of the Wari capital, are filling in many blanks.

The Wari probably first appeared on this stretch of coast around the end of the eighth century. The region lay along what was then the southern edge of the area controlled by the wealthy Moche lords. The region seems to have lacked strong local leaders. Just how the Wari invaders launched their attack is unclear. But a ceremonial drinking cup discovered at El Castillo shows ax-wielding Wari warriors battling coastal defenders armed with spears. At the end of the invasion, the Wari were in firm control. The new lord built a palace at the foot of El Castillo. Over time he and his successors began transforming the steep hill above into a towering temple.

MORE THAN MEETS THE EYE

Covered in nearly a thousand years of rubble and soil, El Castillo today looks like a huge stepped pyramid, like a structure built from the bottom up. From the beginning, though, Giersz suspected that there was more to El Castillo than met the eye. To figure out the building plan, he invited a team of architects to examine the

NOBLE EAR ORNAMENTS
High-ranking Wari women wore ear ornaments. Some are as big as doorknobs.

To rub shoulders in death with members of the royal family, nobles staked out places nearby for tombs of their own. When they used up all of the available space, they built stepped terraces down the slopes of El Castillo.

newly exposed staircases and walls. Their studies revealed something that Giersz had suspected. The Wari engineers had begun construction along the very top of El Castillo and worked their way downward. They adapted this method from elsewhere, says archaeologist Krzysztof Makowski. "In the mountains the Wari made **agricultural terraces**, and they started at the top." As they moved downward, they cut into the slopes to make a tier of platforms.

Along the top of El Castillo the Wari builders carved out an underground chamber. This became the royal tomb. When it was ready for sealing, laborers poured in more than 30 tons of gravel. They capped the entire chamber with a layer of heavy bricks. Then they raised a tower above, with red walls that could be seen for miles around. The Wari ruling class left rich offerings in the small chambers inside. The offerings included finely woven cloth valued more highly than gold and knotted cords used for keeping track of royal goods. They also included the body parts of the Andean condor, a bird closely associated with the Wari nobility. (One title of the Wari emperor may well have been *Mallku*, an ancient Andean word meaning "condor.")

At the center of the tower was a room containing a throne. In later times looters reported that they had found mummies placed in wall niches there. "We are pretty sure this room was used for the **veneration** of the ancestors," says Giersz. It may even have been used for honoring the emperor's mummy, yet to be discovered by the team.

To rub shoulders in death with members of the royal family, nobles staked out places nearby for tombs of their own. When they used up all of the available space, they built stepped terraces down the slopes of El Castillo. They filled the terraces with **funerary** towers and graves.

WOVEN DESIGNS
Pieces of textiles were found throughout El Castillo. The designs and patterns on these textiles provide clues about Wari values and beliefs.

EL CASTILLO
In a maze of chambers, archaeologist Roberto Pimentel Nita examines a find. The dry climate here helps even delicate threads survive in the ground for centuries.

ARRIVAL BY RAFT
A painted figure on a ceramic flask depicts a
Wari lord sitting atop a raft above sea creatures.

So important was El Castillo to the Wari nobles, that they "used every possible local worker," says Giersz. Many of the walls bear human handprints, some left by children as young as 11 or 12 years old.

When the construction ended, likely sometime between A.D. 900 and 1000, an immense red structure loomed over the valley. Though inhabited by the dead, El Castillo sent a powerful political message to the living. The Wari invaders were now the rightful rulers.

THE ROYAL TOMB

In a small walled chamber Wiesław Więckowski bends over a mummified human arm. He brushes sand away from its gaunt fingers. For most of an hour now the Polish archaeologist has been clearing this part of the chamber. He has collected debris from a Wari funerary bundle and looked for the rest of the body. It's slow, delicate work. As he edges his digging tool into a corner of the room, he exposes part of a human leg bone stuck in a jagged hole in the wall. Więckowski frowns in disappointment. Looters, he explains, probably tried to haul the mummy out from a nearby room and in the process pulled it to pieces. "All we can say is that the mummy was a male person and quite old."

A specialist in the study of human remains, Więckowski has begun analyzing the skeletons found in and near the royal tomb. Human soft tissue was not preserved well in the sealed chamber, Więckowski says. But his studies are

GIFT FOR A QUEEN
An artisan carved this drinking cup for a Wari queen from a rare alabaster-like Andean stone.

starting to fill in key details of the lives and deaths of noble Wari women.

Almost all of those buried inside the chamber were women and girls. They likely died over a long period of time, most probably of natural causes. In death the Wari treated them with great respect. Attendants dressed them in richly woven **tunics** and shawls. They painted their faces with a sacred red **pigment**. And they adorned their bodies with gold earrings and crystal necklaces. Then mourners arranged their bodies in the flexed position favored by the Wari and wrapped each in a large cloth to form a funerary bundle.

Their social rank, says Więckowski, mattered as much in death as it did in life. Attendants placed the highest ranked women—perhaps queens or princesses—in three private side chambers in the tomb. The most important, a female of about 60, lay surrounded by rare luxuries: multiple pairs of ear ornaments, a bronze ax, and a silver drinking cup. The archaeologists marveled at her wealth. "This lady, what was she doing?" muses Makowski. "She was weaving with golden instruments, like a true queen."

Beyond, in a large common area, attendants arranged the bundles of less important women along the walls. Beside each, they laid a container the size and shape of a shoebox. In it were all the weaving tools needed to create high-quality cloth. Wari women were expert weavers. They produced cloth finer than that produced by the famous European weavers of the 16th century. The women buried at El Castillo were clearly dedicated to their art.

When the chamber was ready for sealing, attendants brought the last offerings up the slopes of El Castillo: human sacrifices. Więckowski found three children and three young adults. The victims may have been related to the conquered nobles. "If you are the ruler and want people to prove their loyalty . . . you take their children," he says. When the killings were done, attendants threw the bodies into the tomb. The chamber was closed. They placed the wrapped bodies of a young adult male and an older woman at the entrance as guards. Each had lost a left foot, possibly to make sure that they couldn't desert their post.

AN EMERGING STORY

Więckowski is awaiting the results of **DNA** analyses to learn more about the females in the tomb and where they may have come from. But for Giersz the evidence is all beginning to add up to a detailed picture of the Wari invasion of the north coast. "The fact that they built an important temple here, on a prominent piece of land along the former borders of the Moche, strongly suggests that the Wari conquered the region and intended to stay."

In a quiet back room at the Art Museum of Lima, El Castillo's archaeologists beam as they examine some of the newly cleaned finds. For weeks now

NATIONAL GEOGRAPHIC PHOTOGRAPHER **ROBERT CLARK**

HOMETOWN: HAYS, KANSAS
CURRENT RESIDENCE: BROOKLYN, NEW YORK
FIRST NATIONAL GEOGRAPHIC ASSIGNMENT: "LA SALLE'S FINAL VOYAGE," 1995

The gift of a camera from his big brother sent Robert Clark down the path to become the innovative, award-winning photographer he is today. As sports editor for *The Hays Daily*, Clark's brother would have him shoot high school sporting events in and around their hometown.

After spending seven years as a newspaper photographer, Clark joined author Buzz Bissinger in Odessa, Texas, to document the lives of high school football players for the best-selling book *Friday Night Lights*.

Since then he has contributed more than 33 stories, including more than 10 covers, for *National Geographic* magazine. He shot the first digital cover for the magazine in 2003 and his story "Was Darwin Wrong?" received the Picture of the Year award from the National Press Photographers Association.

As the first person to produce a book of images taken with his cell phone, Clark uses photography to tell stories about our rich past as well as our present. He published a book about the evolution of feathers and is working on a book about the evidence of evolution. Clark also continues to photograph archaeological sites and priceless artifacts, like those he took of El Castillo and the Wari treasures pictured in this article.

> *" The fact that they built an important temple here, on a prominent piece of land along the former borders of the Moche, strongly suggests that the Wari conquered the region and intended to stay. "* –Miłosz Giersz

art restorers have been stripping away thick black coating from many of the metal artifacts, revealing shining designs. Cushioned in tissue paper are three golden ear ornaments, each the size of a doorknob and each bearing the image of a winged god or mythical being. Team member Patrycja Prządka-Giersz looks them over in delight. These adornments, she says, "are all different. And we can only see them after conservation."

Looking inside a large cardboard box, Giersz finds one of the team's prize discoveries: a ceramic **pilgrim's flask**. Beautifully painted and decorated, the flask shows a richly dressed Wari lord traveling by raft across coastal waters. The waters teem with whales and other sea creatures. Found among the grave goods of a dead queen at El Castillo, the flask seems to portray an event—partly mythical, partly real—in the history of the north coast: the arrival of an important Wari lord. He was possibly the Wari emperor himself. "And so we are starting to make a story of the Wari emperor who takes to the sea in a raft," says Makowski with a broad smile.

For now it is only a story, an educated guess. But Giersz, who saw the buried outlines of walls where others saw only rubble, still thinks that the tomb of a great Wari lord may lie somewhere in the maze of walls and underground chambers. And if the looters haven't gotten there first, he intends to find it.

THINK ABOUT IT!

1 **Draw Conclusions** State in your own words the questions that Giersz set out to answer. Did he succeed? Explain your answer.

2 **Analyze Cause and Effect** What has made looting such a problem for the archaeologists working at the El Castillo site? Include specific details in your answer.

3 **Find Main Ideas and Details** The Wari were an advanced civilization. What evidence supports this conclusion?

BACKGROUND & VOCABULARY

agricultural terrace *n.* a series of horizontal ridges in a hillside designed to prevent loss of soil for growing crops

aqueduct *n.* (AK-wuh-duhkt) a human-built channel for carrying flowing water, usually from a spring or lake to a city

DNA *n.* an abbreviation for the substance found in a cell that is the basis for hereditary traits

funerary *adj.* (FYOO-nuh-rehr-ee) having to do with burial and funeral practices

pigment *n.* (PIG-muhnt) a substance, generally a powder mixed with a liquid, used for coloring a surface

pilgrim's flask *n.* a bottle-shaped container with a narrow opening, carried by a person traveling to a faraway land

tunic *n.* (TOO-nihk) a simple slip-on garment that comes to the knees or below

veneration *n.* (ven-uh-RAY-shun) the act of showing deep respect or devotion

THE SICÁN REVEALED

WRITTEN BY CATHERINE SHAPIRO

SICÁN LORD
Depicted here in gold, likenesses of this
figure appear frequently in Sicán art.

For generations, looters raided the tombs of northern Peru, searching for gold. In recent years, however, archaeologists have discovered wealth of a different kind—knowledge about a complex culture called the Sicán.

REMARKABLE BURIAL

The man was between 40 and 50 years old when he died. Centuries later, a team of archaeologists found him in a tomb 36 feet beneath the ground in the Lambayeque region of northern Peru. His body had been painted with cinnabar, a type of coloring made from a red mineral. He was turned upside-down. His head had been separated from his body and was placed beside it, right-side up and facing west. On his head was a large, ornate gold mask. Buried near the man in the same carefully arranged tomb were two women and two children.

More than a ton of grave goods including objects made of gold, copper, ceramics, beads, and precious stones surrounded the man. Elaborate gold crowns and headdresses, curious yard-long gloves made of a gold **alloy**, ceremonial knives, and masses of gold jewelry formed just part of this trove. The tomb also contained large numbers of shells, valued as symbols of life-sustaining water. Much of the remaining space was filled with scrap metal left over from the process of crafting the decorative grave goods.

This was the scene that greeted archaeologist Izumi Shimada and his team when they excavated the site known as the East Tomb from 1991 to 1992. Shimada had been studying the people who dug this grave, the Sicán, since 1978. At that time, he founded the Sicán Archaeological Project. Before Shimada began his study, the Sicán were largely unknown.

For years, collectors have prized masks, ceremonial knives, and other precious artifacts from Peru's early history. Even knowledgeable collectors assumed that most of these objects were made by the Inca. Others erroneously accredited them to the Chimú, who were rivals of the Inca. In fact, many of these artifacts are older than their owners believe. They were likely created by the Sicán, who lived in northern Peru from around A.D. 800 to 1400.

Looting is one reason the Sicán culture remained **obscure** for so long. Some private collectors are willing to pay top dollar for objects from Peru's pre-Columbian era—especially ones made from gold and other precious metals. The problem with looted artifacts is that they yield little information about the people who made them. Much of what researchers can learn about past cultures comes from viewing the objects they find in context. That is, they take note of where objects are found—in a grave, for example, or in a ruined temple. They consider which objects are found together and how they relate to each other. These details help researchers draw conclusions about the people who used the artifacts—how they lived, what they believed, and how they related to other cultures.

The main Sicán archaeological site had been looted for many years when Shimada began his work there. Looters would dig deep holes and tunnels in search of treasure. In the 1960s, one enterprising thief brought in a bulldozer to scrape away the surface soil. When Shimada began working at the site in 1978, he looked at aerial photos of the land and counted more than 100,000 looters' holes.

"Professional looters take custom orders for specific items and literally destroy everything in archaeological sites (especially tombs) to find a particular item," Shimada said. He was speaking at the opening of the *Peruvian Gold: Ancient Treasures Unearthed* exhibition at the National Geographic Museum in 2014, where several of the Sicán artifacts he uncovered were displayed.

The good news is that many governments take the risks of looting very seriously. In 2001, the Peruvian government created the Pómac Forest Historical Sanctuary, a protected area that includes the Sicán site.

SICÁN CULTURE AND RELIGION

The Sicán culture rose and flourished in the fertile Lambayeque region of Peru. The land was watered by rivers that arose in the Andes Mountains and by a network of irrigation canals. The Sicán people grew a variety of crops, including corn, squash, peppers, and tomatoes. They raised llamas, guinea pigs, and hairless dogs for meat, and they supplemented their diets with fish from the nearby Pacific Ocean.

The main religious center of the region was located in the valley of the La Leche River. Like the culture it personifies, this site is called Sicán. Evidence suggests that Sicán was not the political capital. Rather, it was a gathering place for both public and private ceremonies. Here, priests performed sacred rituals and members of the society's elite were buried. The core area of the site covers nearly 400 acres and is dominated by 12 enormous platform mounds, called *huacas*. Some mounds reach as high as 130 feet and have bases that measure 330 square feet.

The mounds were constructed by building platforms one upon another. Each platform consisted of cells made of adobe walls and formed into a perfect lattice, or grid, pattern. The cells were filled with trash and any other materials that were handy before the next platform was built on top. At the top of each mound was a temple. At the bases of the mounds, and sometimes beneath them, were the graves of Sicán's nobles and other elite. The East Tomb was one of these. It was found at the base of a mound called Huaca Loro.

Researchers believe the Sicán worshipped a **deity**, or god, known today as the Sicán Deity. Images of this god appear frequently on masks, goblets, ceramics, textiles, and other items used for religious ceremonies. The Sicán Deity is portrayed as a man with bird-like features such as wings, a beaked nose, and talons on his feet.

REPEATING MOTIFS
Symbols of waves and birds like the ones in the mural art above also appear on this gold crown, mounted on modern black cloth.

Sometimes he is shown standing above the ocean with the sun and moon on either side of him. At times he is also shown with either nocturnal animals or animals most commonly seen at the start of summer. Researchers theorize that these elements may symbolize opposing concepts, such as death and life. Frequently, too, the deity has teardrops on his face. These may stand for water, which was crucial to both life and farming.

METAL MASTERS

The Sicán people may have been wonderful farmers, but they made their true mark as metalworkers. The Sicán culture reached its height during the period known as the Middle Sicán era, between A.D. 900 and 1100. During this time, Sicán metalworkers produced a rich variety of artifacts made from bronze, copper, and gold alloys. According to Shimada, the Sicán's use of new alloys "ushered the bronze age into northern Peru."

The Sicán crafters were masters of sheet metal. This demanding technique involved

SICÁN WORLDVIEW
Natural elements played a central role in the Sicán worldview. This reconstructed wall mural shows the Sicán Deity (center) standing in the Pacific Ocean, surrounded by waves and fish, and flanked by the sun and moon.

pounding metal **ingots** into uniformly thin sheets, using stone hammers and **anvils**. The process was painstaking. It required tremendous skill to avoid making cracks in the metal.

Many of the objects in the East Tomb reflect the best of Sicán sheet-metal craftsmanship. For example, two strips of metal found in the grave are 6.5 feet long and just .006 inches thick. The mask on the man's head offers a striking example of the beauty and creative vision that accompanied the crafters' skill. It was formed from a sheet of gold alloy .02 inches thick, yet it is strong enough to support the many decorations that adorn it. When worn in ceremony, the decorated mask was an amazing display of color, sound, and motion as its different parts shined, rang, and danced.

MUSICAL HEADBAND
This gold headband found in the East Tomb was worn by one of the women who accompanied the man buried there. Notice the dangling pieces that would make sounds as the woman moved.

EL TOCADO

Curator Fred Hiebert tells the story of the centerpiece of the Peruvian Gold: Ancient Treasures Unearthed *exhibition, a gold headdress named "El Tocado," and its connection to a much older artifact.*

The artifact to the left is named El Tocado, which means "The Headdress." It was excavated in 1991 by my professor, Izumi Shimada, who kept it a secret from his students. He didn't tell us what he was doing because he knew his site was in danger if he started telling everybody about the gold. We didn't know where he went. But he was excavating this incredible headdress—the largest pre-Columbian headdress ever found in Peru.

The El Tocado headdress is about four feet tall, weighs about 25 pounds, and is made up of several different parts. First, there is the Sicán Lord's gold mask **1** , painted with red. The red comes from cinnabar, a sacred color and material. The mask has inlays of amber, which create these glowing eyes. On either side of the mask, there are magnificent gold ear spools **2** , intricately designed and very heavy.

A forehead ornament in the shape of a vampire bat **3** sits above the mask. This bat has moveable parts, including its tongue, used for lapping up blood.

Finally, above the bat, there is whole series of golden feathers **4** creating an amazing display, almost gaudy. The feathers radiate from the U-shaped head piece like rays of the sun. Professor Shimada told us that actual feathers from Amazonian birds were placed outside of those golden feathers. We didn't know quite what to make of this extraordinary headdress.

THE LONGEVITY OF CULTURE

El Tocado dates from A.D. 900 to 1100. The ceramic drinking vessel below (also featured on page 24) is easily dated 1,000 years earlier. But if you look carefully at the central figure you can see exactly the same figure that appears on the headdress. He's wearing a mask that has big ear spools almost exactly the same as those that appear on the Sicán Lord's mask, and above the mask is a bat forehead ornament.

It's as if in this ceramic we're seeing the same person and the same story, a mythical story being passed down. It's a real lesson about the longevity of culture, that 1,000 years earlier a different society is depicting the same story, the same picture of an important person wearing a golden mask adorned with ear spools and a vampire bat. That's pretty cool.

BANCO CENTRAL DE RESERVA DEL PERÚ, Lima, Perú.

THE ARTIFACTS SPEAK

The Sicán metal artifacts offer more than shiny treasures for us to admire. They give researchers like Shimada important insights into Sicán culture. Shimada and his team excavated several tombs at Sicán, including some that were much less elaborate than the East Tomb. By studying the grave goods, the archaeologists were able to conclude that certain metals were associated with different social classes. Those at the top of society had items made of gold and alloys with a high gold content. The lesser elite could not possess pure gold but were allowed to have items made of alloys with a high gold content. Commoners were limited to less valuable metals such as bronze.

The quantity and quality of metals in the elite tombs also led Shimada to some conclusions about the wealth and organization of the Sicán culture. For example, a study of the grave goods revealed different levels of craftsmanship. Shimada believes some items were made by apprentice metalworkers under the supervision of master crafters. This implies a highly organized system of workshops, in which masters trained youths in the delicate art of metalworking. It is likely, too, that crafters specialized in different areas or types of metalwork.

The tomb metals also give an indication of the impressive resources commanded by the Sicán elite. Jo Ann Griffin, a goldsmith and expert in pre-Columbian metal techniques, was able to create a sheet of gold using only Sicán tools and methods. She found that it took her a full day and a half to hammer a one-ounce nugget of gold into a thin sheet like those produced by the Sicán crafters.

Based on this experiment, Shimada calculated that the sheet metal in just the East Tomb alone represents tens of thousands of work hours. Add to that the effort and resources needed to acquire the base metals to make the alloys. Then factor in the enormous amounts of hardwood needed to burn in the forges. It's impossible to put a dollar amount on the total. Still, the calculation points to a very wealthy nobility that could command the work of many people.

The heyday of the Sicán culture came to an end in the 11th century. Between 1020 and 1050, the Lambayeque region suffered a drought

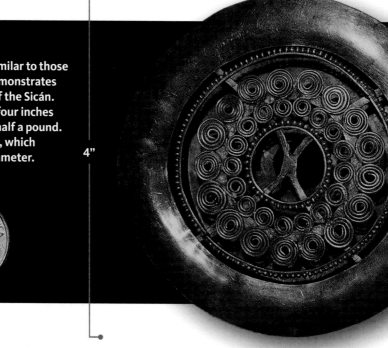

EXPERT GOLDSMITHING
The detail on this gold ear spool, similar to those found on the Sicán Lord's mask, demonstrates the extraordinary craftsmanship of the Sicán. Note the size of the ear spool: it is four inches in diameter and it weighs nearly a half a pound. Compare the ear spool to a quarter, which measures just under one inch in diameter.

4"

.995"

"We didn't know quite what to make of this extraordinary headdress."
– Fred Hiebert

EXCAVATING THE MASK
The Sicán Lord's Mask, part of El Tocado, sits in a box patiently as Izumi Shimada (left) continues his excavation of the East Tomb.

that lasted three decades. A massive flood drowned the fields around Sicán and wrecked the irrigation networks. Soon after, Sicán itself was deliberately burned and then abandoned. Interestingly, when the capital was deserted, artists and crafters stopped portraying the Sicán Deity in their works.

The center of Sicán culture moved to a different site, called Túcume. There, the rulers built gigantic platform mounds and artisans continued to produce ritual objects. But the quality of the artwork had diminished, and it never recovered. Sometime around 1375, the Lambayeque region was conquered by the Chimú, and the Sicán era had come to an end.

In the centuries that followed, other cultures arose, and the Spanish came to Peru. The world moved on. The treasures of the Sicán culture remained hidden from sight, disturbed only by looters in search of profitable goods. Today, these precious artifacts have found a safe home. At the request of the Peruvian government, Izumi Shimada designed the Sicán National Museum in Ferreñafe, Peru. There, visitors can marvel at the Sicán artifacts and rediscover the sophisticated culture that flowered 1,000 years ago between the Andes Mountains and the Pacific Ocean.

THINK ABOUT IT! |||||||||||||||||||||||||||||

1 **Analyze Cause and Effect** How did nature and geography shape the development and fate of the Sicán culture?

2 **Analyze Visuals** Choose one artifact shown in the photos. How does this artifact illustrate some of the concepts described in the article?

BACKGROUND & VOCABULARY

alloy *n.* (AL-oy) a metal made by mixing two or more metals together

anvil *n.* (AN-vuhl) a heavy iron or stone block on which a piece of heated metal is placed to be hammered into shape

deity *n.* (DEE-uh-tee) a god or supernatural being

ingot *n.* (EEN-guht) a solid piece of metal that has been formed into a brick-like shape

obscure *adj.* (uhb-SCYOOR) poorly known; difficult to know

Lofty Ambitions of the INCA

Adapted from "Lofty Ambitions of the Inca," by Heather Pringle, in *National Geographic*, April 2011

MOUNTAINTOP CITY
Perched high in the Peruvian Andes, Machu Picchu shows the Inca's masterful building skills with its precision-cut stones and layers of terraces.

National Geographic writer Heather Pringle specializes in archaeological subjects. In this article, she describes how the Inca conquered kingdoms, sculpted mountains, and built a mighty empire.

TRACING INCA ORIGINS

On the remote Peruvian island of Taquile, in the middle of the great Lake Titicaca, hundreds of people stand on the plaza in silence, listening to a Roman Catholic priest recite a prayer. Descended in part from Inca colonists sent here more than 500 years ago, the inhabitants of Taquile keep the old ways. They weave brilliantly colored cloth and speak the old language of the Inca. They tend their fields as they have for centuries. On festival days they gather in the plaza to dance to the sound of wooden pipes and drums.

The names of Inca rulers still ring with power and ambition, centuries after their passing. For example, Viracocha Inca means "Creator God Ruler" and Pachacutec Inca Yupanqui means "He Who Remakes the World." Remake the world they did. Rising from obscurity in Peru's Cusco Valley during the 13th century, a royal Inca dynasty created the largest pre-Columbian empire in the New World. To extend their domain, they preferred to charm, bribe, or intimidate their rivals. But if necessary, they used deadly force.

Until recently, scholars didn't know much about the lives of Inca kings. The only histories, told by Inca nobles to the Spanish conquistadores soon after their arrival in the 1500s, were more flattering than factual. The Inca had no system of writing, as the Maya did. Any portraits that Inca artists may have made of their rulers were lost. The royal palaces of Cusco, the Inca capital, were swiftly destroyed by the Spaniards. A Spanish colonial city was built on Cusco's ruins, and the Inca past was all but buried. In the early 1980s, civil unrest broke out in the Peruvian Andes. For safety reasons, few archaeologists worked in the Inca heartland for more than a decade.

But now they are making up for lost time. Archaeologists are discovering thousands of previously unknown sites in the rugged mountains near Cusco. These discoveries shed new light on the origins of the Inca dynasty. Studying colonial documents, researchers are finding the lost estates of Inca rulers. They are piecing together the complex relationships of imperial households and finding evidence of the wars Inca kings fought. Often their weapon was psychological warfare, not raw power. Rulers used every means to pull neighboring groups into their empire. Their unmatched ability to triumph on the battlefield and to build a civilization sent a clear message, says archaeologist Dennis Ogburn: "I think they were saying, 'We are the most powerful people in the world, so don't even think of messing with us.'"

AN EMPIRE TAKES SHAPE

On a sun-washed July afternoon, archaeologist Brian Bauer stands in the plaza of the sprawling Inca ceremonial site of Maukallacta (maw-kah-LAHK-tah), south of Cusco. He points to a tall rock formation to the east. Carved into its rugged summit are massive steps, part of a major Inca shrine. About 500 years ago, Bauer says, pilgrims journeyed here to worship. It was one of the most sacred places in the empire. It was believed to be the birthplace of the Inca dynasty.

Bauer first came to Maukallacta in the early 1980s. His dream was to uncover the origins of the Inca Empire. At the time most historians believed that a young Andean named Pachacutec became the first Inca king in the early 1400s. Supposedly, Pachacutec created a mighty empire in one generation. Bauer didn't buy it, however.

AMBITION UNBOUND

In just a few generations, the Inca conquered 300,000 square miles along South America's western coast.

1 ca 1400
Having subdued their neighbors, Inca kings launch their first conquests beyond the Cusco region.

2 ca 1470
Pushing to the coast, the Inca defeat the Chimú Empire and carry off many Chimú artisans.

3 ca 1500
Turning south, the Inca capture a vast territory, extending their reach to the edge of Patagonia.

4 by 1532
In a final thrust along the eastern slope of the Andes, the Inca expand farther into the Amazon Basin.

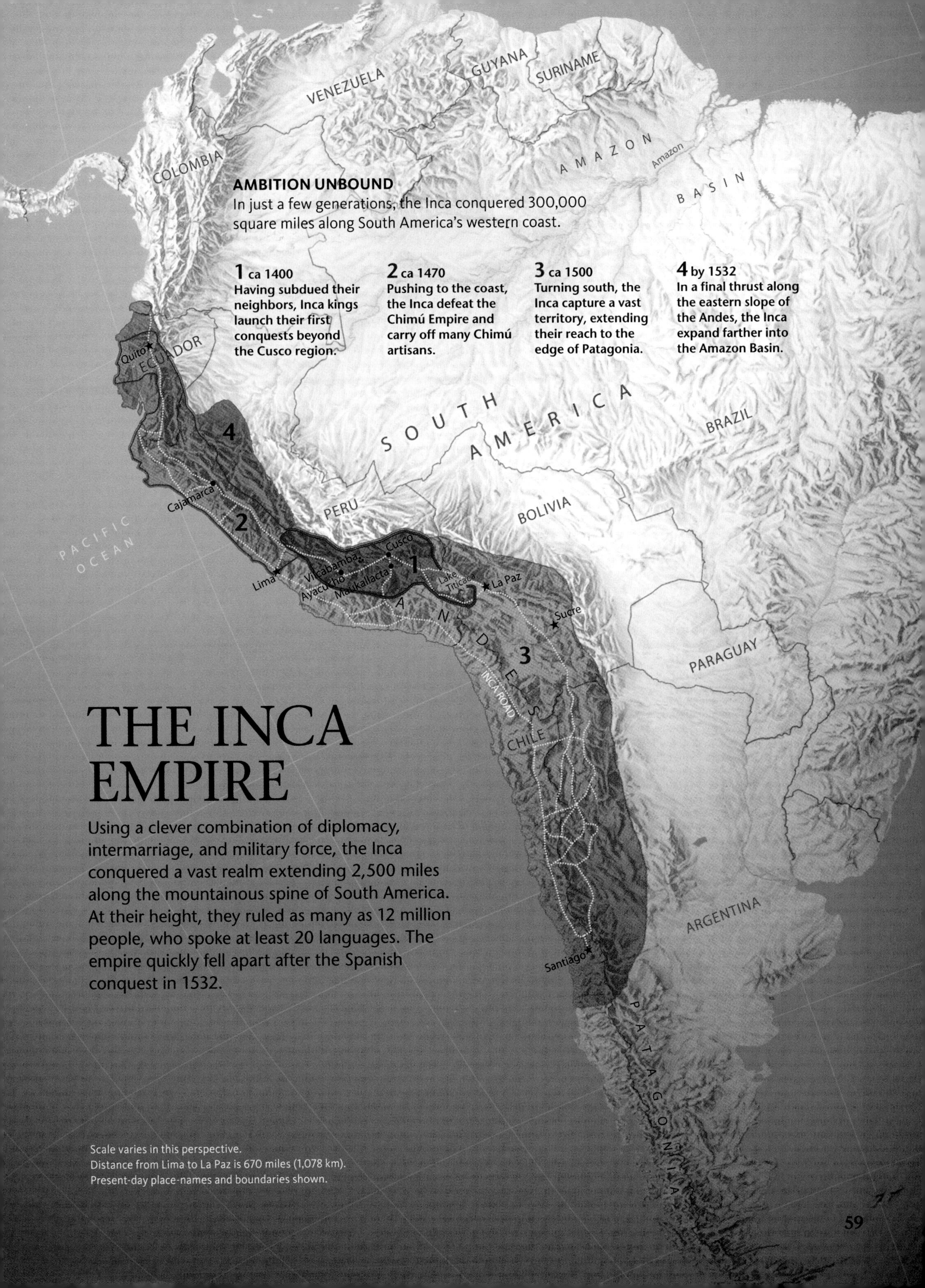

THE INCA EMPIRE

Using a clever combination of diplomacy, intermarriage, and military force, the Inca conquered a vast realm extending 2,500 miles along the mountainous spine of South America. At their height, they ruled as many as 12 million people, who spoke at least 20 languages. The empire quickly fell apart after the Spanish conquest in 1532.

Scale varies in this perspective.
Distance from Lima to La Paz is 670 miles (1,078 km).
Present-day place-names and boundaries shown.

VENEZUELA

GUYANA

SURINAME

COLOMBIA

A M A Z O N

B A S I N

Amazon

Quito

ECUADOR

S O U T H

A M E R I C A

BRAZIL

Cajamarca

PERU

BOLIVIA

PACIFIC
OCEAN

Lima
Vilcabamba
Ayacucho
Maukallacta
Cusco
Lake
Titicaca
La Paz

Sucre

A
N
D
E
S

INCA ROAD

CHILE

PARAGUAY

ARGENTINA

Santiago

P
A
T
A
G
O
N
I
A

He believed that the Inca dynasty had deeper roots, and Maukallacta seemed the logical place to look for them. To his surprise, two seasons of digging turned up no trace of Inca lords.

So Bauer moved north, to the Cusco Valley. With colleague R. Alan Covey and a team of Peruvian assistants, he marched up and down the steep mountain slopes for four field seasons. They were determined to record every piece of pottery or toppled stone wall they saw. Their hard work paid off. Bauer and his team eventually discovered thousands of new Inca sites. The evidence showed that an Inca state had risen much earlier than previously thought—sometime between 1200 and 1300.

The former rulers of the region, the mighty Wari lords, had fallen by 1100. One major cause was a severe drought that lasted for a century or more. In the later turmoil, local chiefs across the Peruvian highlands battled over scarce water. They led raiders into neighboring villages in search of food. Hordes of refugees fled to frigid mountain hideouts, often above 13,000 feet. In the fertile valley around Cusco, however, Inca farmers stood their ground. Instead of warring among themselves, Inca villages united into a small state capable of defending itself.

Between 1150 and 1300, the Inca around Cusco benefitted from a major warming trend. As temperatures climbed, Inca farmers moved 800 to 1,000 feet up the slopes. They built agricultural terraces, irrigated their fields, and enjoyed record harvests. Researcher Alex Chepstow-Lusty has been studying the region's past climate. "These surpluses," says Chepstow-Lusty, allowed the Inca to "free up many people for other roles, whether building roads or maintaining a large army."

Eventually, Inca rulers commanded the largest army in the area. With this big stick, Inca kings began eyeing the lands and resources of others. They married the daughters of neighboring lords, and gave generously to their new allies. When a rival lord rejected their advances or stirred up trouble, they used their military might. One by one, local lords gave in. In the end, there was only one mighty state and one capital, the sacred city of Cusco.

Encouraged by their success, Inca kings set their sights farther afield. The rich lands surrounding Lake Titicaca were too tempting to resist. Sometime after 1400, one of the greatest Inca rulers, Pachacutec Inca Yupanqui, began planning his conquest of the south. It was the dawn of the Inca Empire.

INCA WARFARE STRATEGIES

Gathered on a high Peruvian plain near Lake Titicaca in the mid-1400s, the Colla forces were heavily armed. They dared the Inca invaders to attack. Pachacutec looked over the enemy ranks in silence, preparing for the great battle ahead. The lords of the Titicaca region proudly ruled as many as 400,000 people. Their lands were productive, gold and silver were plentiful in the mountains, and herds of alpacas and llamas grazed in the meadows.

Military success in the Andes depended on alpacas and llamas. They were hardy mountain animals. One llama alone could carry 70 pounds of gear, and both alpacas and llamas provided

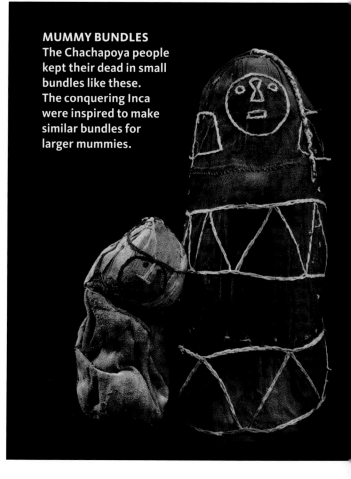

MUMMY BUNDLES
The Chachapoya people kept their dead in small bundles like these. The conquering Inca were inspired to make similar bundles for larger mummies.

meat, leather, and wool. They were food, clothing, and transportation, all rolled into one. The Inca king realized he must conquer the Titicaca lords who owned these vast herds. Otherwise he would live in fear that they would come to conquer him.

Seated on a shimmering litter, Pachacutec issued the order to attack. Playing war drums and **panpipes** carved from the bones of enemies, his soldiers advanced toward the Colla army. Then both sides charged. When the battle was over, Colla bodies littered the field.

In the years that followed, Pachacutec and his descendants defeated all the southern lords. "The conquest of the Titicaca Basin was the jewel in the crown of the Inca Empire," says archaeologist Charles Stanish. However, military victory was only the beginning. The next step was to gain control of the people.

If an area rebelled, Inca kings moved their populations, sending troublemakers to the Inca heartland and replacing them with loyal subjects. Residents of remote villages were resettled to new Inca-controlled towns located along Inca-built roads. These roads were needed for moving Inca troops. Inca governors ordered the construction of roadside storehouses for troops and forced locals to supply them. "The Inca were the organizational geniuses of the Americas," says Stanish.

Under Inca rule, Andean civilization thrived. Engineers built a network of highways. Stone workers built architectural masterpieces such as Machu Picchu, which continues to awe visitors today. Farmers learned to grow some 70 different high-altitude crops. They often had as much as three to seven years' worth of food in storage. Officials mastered the art of inventory control. They used an Andean coding method—colored and knotted cords known as *quipus*—to track storehouse contents.

By the time the Inca king Huayna Capac took power around 1493, little was beyond his reach.

EXPOSED BY LOOTERS
Five centuries ago, these mummies were bound into bundles, which resulted in twisted poses but made them easier to carry. Modern looters tore off their wrappings, hoping to find gold.

COLORFUL CLOTHING
The clothing these women are wearing reflects Peru's history. Their shawls follow an Inca tradition, but their upturned hats and full skirts were inspired by the Spanish.

To build a grand new capital in Ecuador, Huayna Capac ordered huge stone blocks brought from Cusco, nearly a thousand miles away up and down steep mountain roads. He put more than 4,500 defiant subjects to work hauling the blocks. In the Inca heartland, laborers worked on the estate of the royal family.

At the king's command, the Urubamba River was moved to the southern side of the valley. In order to do so, workers leveled hills and drained marshes. They planted corn and other crops such as cotton, peanuts, and hot peppers. In the center of the estate, they laid stones and bricks for Huayna Capac's new country palace,

Quispiguanca (KEE-spee-gwahn-kah). Located on the edge of the modern town of Urubamba, Quispiguanca has one of the warmest climates in the region. The Inca royal family must have enjoyed their escape from the cold of Cusco.

The estate's surviving walls enclose a royal compound that once covered more than 12 acres.

Surrounded by parks and gardens, Quispiguanca was a place for a warrior-king to unwind after battle. The grounds included a hidden lodge and a forest for hunting deer. In the fields hundreds of workers cleared irrigation channels, maintained terrace walls, and grew corn and other crops. These provided Huayna Capac with harvests bountiful enough to entertain his subjects royally during festivals.

Quispiguanca was not the only great estate. An Inca king inherited little more than his title, so he had to build his city palace and country home for himself. To date, archaeologists have located ruins of roughly a dozen Inca royal estates.

Even after Inca kings died, they remained the powers behind the throne. "The ancestors were a key element of Andean life," says Sonia Guillén, director of Peru's Museo Leymebamba. When Huayna Capac died in Ecuador around 1527, his body was mummified and carried back to Cusco.

A king's death did not keep members of the royal family from visiting him. They often sought his opinion on vital matters, following the advice spoken by an **oracle** sitting at his side. Years after his death, Huayna Capac remained the owner of Quispiguanca and the surrounding estate. Indeed, tradition demanded that its harvest was to support his mummy, servants, wives, and descendants in style for eternity.

SYMBOLS OF POWER

During the rainy season in 1533, a favorable time for a coronation, thousands of people packed into the main plaza of Cusco to celebrate the arrival of their new teenage king. Two years earlier, foreign invaders had landed in the north. Metal-clad and bearing lethal new weapons, the Spaniards had trekked to the northern Inca town of Cajamarca. There they took the Inca king, Atahuallpa, prisoner. Eight months later, they murdered him. Then their leader, Francisco Pizarro, picked a young prince, Manco Inca Yupanqui, to rule as a **puppet king**.

In the far distance, voices echoed through the streets, singing songs of praise. Celebrants knew their new king was about to enter the square. Following traditional custom, Manco Inca was accompanied by his mummified ancestors, each richly dressed and seated upon a splendid litter.

SALT HARVEST
The pools of mineral-laden water at Maras produce salt by evaporation, as they did for the Inca several hundred years ago.

The mummies reminded everyone that Manco Inca came from a long line of kings.

In the months that followed, the Spanish invaders seized the palaces of Cusco and the country estates, angering Manco Inca. In 1536 he tried to drive them from his land. When his army was defeated, he fled Cusco for the jungle. From there, he launched guerrilla attacks until finally subdued in 1572.

In the confusion of those decades, the Inca's extensive network of roads, storehouses, and estates fell into ruin. As the empire crumbled, the Inca and their descendants made a brave attempt to preserve the symbols of imperial power. Servants collected and hid the bodies of the sacred kings and worshipped them in secret, defying the Spanish priests. In 1559 Cusco's chief magistrate decided to stamp out this idol worship. He launched an official search for the bodies, questioning hundreds. He seized the remains of 11 Inca kings and several queens.

For a time colonial officials in Lima displayed the mummies of several royals as curiosities in a Lima hospital that admitted only European patients. But the bodies began to deteriorate in the damp coastal air. So Spanish officials secretly buried the Inca kings in Lima, far from the Andes and the people who worshipped them.

In 2001 Brian Bauer and two Peruvian colleagues searched for the mummies of the Inca kings. They hoped to right a historic wrong and to restore an important part of Peruvian heritage.

"Can you imagine," Bauer asks, "how American citizens would feel if the British had taken the bodies of the first several presidents back to London during the War of 1812?"

For months Bauer and his colleagues studied old architectural plans of the hospital where the mummies were last seen. The team identified several possible burial sites. Using ground-penetrating radar, they scanned likely areas, turning up what seemed to be an underground crypt. Bauer and his colleagues were thrilled.

When they finally dug down and opened the door of the dusty chamber, they were crushed. The crypt lay empty. Quite possibly, says Bauer, workmen removed the contents while repairing the hospital after an earthquake. Today no one can say where Peru's greatest kings lie. Bauer concludes, "The fate of the royal Inca mummies remains unknown."

THINK ABOUT IT! |||||||||||||||||||||||||||||||||

1 **Analyze Cause and Effect** How were the civilizations of the Wari and Inca affected by changes in climate?

2 **Explain** The Inca are described as "the organizational geniuses of the Americas." Explain how evidence from the article supports this statement.

BACKGROUND & VOCABULARY

oracle *n.* (AWR-uh-kuhl) a person such as a priest or priestess through whom the gods were believed to speak

panpipe *n.* (PAN-pyp) a musical wind instrument made of several tubes of different lengths

puppet king *n.* a ruler with no real power who is controlled by another person or country

BINGHAM THE EXPLORER
From his camp at Machu Picchu,
Bingham set out to study one of
the few Inca sites untouched by
Spanish invaders.

FINDING MACHU PICCHU

Adapted from "Finding Machu Picchu," by
Heather Pringle, in *National Geographic*, April 2011

In the early 1900s, Hiram Bingham III made various trips to South America, following historic routes and exploring the lands of past civilizations. In his travels, he came across many ruins. But none of them would prove to be as spectacular—and as untouched—as the city of Machu Picchu.

A CLIMB ON "OLD MOUNTAIN"

On hands and knees, three men crawled up a steep mountain slope in the Peruvian Andes. It was the morning of July 24, 1911. One of the men was Hiram Bingham III, a 35-year-old assistant professor of Latin American history at Yale University. Early that morning, he had set out from his expedition camp on the Urubamba River with two Peruvian companions. His goal was to see if reports of ruins on a towering ridge high in the mountains were true. The ridge was known as Machu Picchu, which means "old mountain" in the Inca language.

Nearly 2,000 feet above the valley floor, the climbers met two farmers. The men told Bingham that the rumored ruins lay close at hand. Tired and frustrated, Bingham was doubtful. But the men insisted, and sent a young boy along to lead the way. When Bingham finally reached the site, he stared in astonishment. Rising out of the dense **undergrowth** was a maze of terraces and walls. It was an Inca ghost town hidden from the outside world—including plundering Spanish conquerors—for nearly 400 years. "It seemed like an unbelievable dream," he later wrote. "What could this place be?"

A CITY REVEALED
After months of clearing centuries of overgrowth, Machu Picchu's splendor emerged.

STUDYING MACHU PICCHU

Hiram Bingham later acknowledged that he was not the first person to discover Machu Picchu. A Peruvian farmer had carved his name on one of its walls nearly a decade earlier. Bingham, however, was the first to study the site scientifically.

With financial support from Yale University and the National Geographic Society, Bingham returned to the site with a team of colleagues and assistants. Bingham and his crew worked hard to uncover the mountaintop city. They cleared the vegetation in order to reclaim the peak. They carefully mapped and photographed every part of the city. Bingham also collected thousands of artifacts, which he then shipped to Yale's Peabody Museum of Natural History in New Haven, Connecticut.

As news of the "lost city" spread, scholars tried to figure out just what kind of place Machu Picchu was. Was it a fortress, or maybe a ceremonial site? For many decades no one really knew. A breakthrough came in the 1980s when historians found a dusty legal document from 1568, less than 40 years after the Spanish conquest of Peru.

The document was a **petition** to the Spanish court by descendants of the ruler Pachacutec Inca Yupanqui. In it, the descendants stated that their royal ancestor had owned lands at a place called Picchu. The place was very close to where Machu Picchu sits today. Later studies of the site's architecture and artifacts suggest that Pachacutec lived in comfort at this mountaintop retreat. He ate his meals from silver plates, washed in a private stone bath, and relaxed in an orchid-scented garden.

THE CAMERA

- Bingham always carried his Kodak 3A Special camera on expeditions.

- He only shot one roll of film on his first expedition to Machu Picchu.

- On photographing the "lost city" that first day, Bingham said, "I had a good camera and the sun was shining."

RETURN OF THE ARTIFACTS

In time, the fate of the artifacts Bingham collected during his three expeditions became the source of a bitter dispute between the Peruvian government and Yale University. In 2011, as the 100th anniversary of Bingham's discovery drew near, Yale announced that it would return all the artifacts to Peru.

Today this icon of the Inca world continues to **beckon** explorers and tourists. Each day nearly 2,000 people make their way up the ridge and behold the sight that caused Bingham to exclaim, "It fairly took my breath away."

THINK ABOUT IT! ||||||||||||||||||||||||||||||||

1 Pose and Answer Questions Think of a question you would have liked to ask Bingham about the first time he saw Machu Picchu.

2 Summarize In your own words, explain why so many people continue to visit Machu Picchu every day.

3 Evaluate Today, scholars believe it is important for cultural artifacts to remain in their countries of origin. How would you explain their position?

BACKGROUND & VOCABULARY

beckon *v.* (BEH-kuhn) to encourage or invite someone to follow or visit

petition *n.* (puh-TIH-shuhn) a formal written request to an official person or body of people, such as a royal court

undergrowth *n.* the low growth on a forest floor such as seedlings, saplings, bushes, shrubs, and other plants

Peru's Ice Maidens

Adapted from "Peru's Ice Maidens: Unwrapping the Secrets," by Johan Reinhard, in *National Geographic*, June 1996

FROZEN IN TIME
The frigid, dry mountain air preserved this ice maiden's skin, hair, and clothing for hundreds of years.

National Geographic Explorer Johan Reinhard narrates the unprecedented find of the frozen graves of the ice maidens who were sacrificed on a Peruvian mountain 500 years earlier. The mummies reveal details of their last days, and provide insights into the Inca at the height of their power.

THE GIRL ATOP AMPATO

She had long dark hair, a thin, graceful neck, and well-muscled arms. When she gave her young life to the mountain god of Nevado Ampato, the Inca maiden was dressed in colorful garments of fine alpaca wool. She died five centuries ago on the summit of Ampato, a 20,700-foot volcano in the Peruvian Andes, in a ritual ceremony led by a small group of Inca priests.

Ampato was sacred to the Inca. As a god who brought life-giving water and good harvests, Ampato was given the highest tribute: the sacrifice of one of the Inca's own people.

Miguel Zárate, my Peruvian climbing partner, and I were unaware of this as we slogged up the ash-covered ridge that leads to Ampato's summit. It was September 8, 1995, and recent eruptions of a nearby volcano, Nevado Sabancaya, had spewed ash, blanketing Ampato.

I stopped to take notes. Miguel kept moving. Then I heard a whistle and saw his ice ax raised in the air. When I reached him, he pointed to a tiny fan of reddish feathers protruding from a nearby slope. We both knew instantly that they were part of a headdress of the sort found on Inca ceremonial statuettes. The feather tips were nearly perfect, so they must have been exposed only briefly to the elements.

Looking around, we saw stones that had formed part of an Inca ceremonial platform. It had been perched above gullies that dropped out of sight to an ice-covered crater 200 feet below. We climbed down into it and noticed what appeared to be the cloth bundle of a mummy.

This seemed so unlikely that Miguel said, "Maybe it's a climber's backpack." As we drew closer, we saw that the object, wrapped tightly in textiles, was indeed an Inca mummy. I felt a jolt of excitement. In 15 years I'd climbed more than a hundred peaks in the Andes and conducted various archaeological excavations, but not once seen a mummy bundle like this on a mountain.

Near the mummy were pieces of cloth, a miniature female figurine made of **spondylus shell**, llama bones, pieces of pottery, and two cloth bags containing corn kernels and a corncob. After I'd photographed these objects, Miguel used his ax to free the mummy from its icy pedestal. He turned it on its side and we found ourselves looking into the face of an Inca girl.

Only a very few frozen mummies have been found anywhere in the Andes—and none is a female. This girl, in her early teens, must have been ritually sacrificed and buried on the summit of Ampato. Sometime after 1993, when the summit ridge began disintegrating, ice and rock slid downslope, taking with it the mummy and her tomb. The tomb broke up and was lost, leaving only traces of the summit platform.

We faced a dilemma. If we left the mummy, the sun and volcanic ash would damage her further, and looters could rob the site. What's more, a heavy snowfall could bury the summit.

There seemed no alternative but to carry the mummy and as many artifacts as we could down the mountain. We'd then take her the hundred miles to the archaeology department at Catholic University in Arequipa, my academic base in Peru. There, in a freezer, she'd be safe.

A REMARKABLE FIND

"It's a discovery of worldwide importance—she's better preserved than the Iceman," was Konrad Spindler's reaction when he came to Arequipa to examine the mummy. Spindler heads the continuing studies in Austria of the famous Tyrolean "Iceman."

We know that the Inca came to this region after 1450 and the Spanish conquest occurred in 1532. Therefore, we can assume that the girl, nicknamed Juanita, died about 500 years ago. This makes her a baby compared with the Iceman, who is about 5,000 years old. Some Chinchorro mummies from coastal Chile date back 7,000 years.

The intact body tissues and organs of naturally mummified, frozen bodies contain a lot of biological information. Future studies of the mummy may reveal how she died. Her DNA should enable us to identify not only the region she came from but also who her living relatives are. Analysis of her stomach contents may yield insights about the Inca diet. A feather-covered bag we found near her held coca leaves. The leaves were sacred offerings 500 years ago and still are today. Using modern techniques of biochemical analysis, we hope to locate the actual valley where those plants grew.

The girl's clothes are no less remarkable—richly patterned, dazzling textiles that will serve as the model for future depictions of the way noble Inca women dressed. Some of the garments appear too big for her. Perhaps the Inca perceived she would exist in the afterlife as an adult. When William Conklin, an expert on pre-Columbian textiles at the National Gallery of Art in Washington, D.C., saw her *lliclla*—a bright red-and-white shawl beneath the outer wrappings—he declared it "the finest Inca woman's textile in the world."

As a mountaineer and an anthropologist, I have long been drawn to the study of mountain worship. Artifacts in high-altitude sites can be exceptionally well preserved because of the cold conditions. These places also have a better chance of being untouched by looters. By examining objects in their proper contexts, we gain a deeper understanding of ancient customs and beliefs.

RESCUING THE MUMMY
Climber Miguel Zárate sees the face of the Inca maiden mummy for the first time.

Exploring another site below Ampato's summit, we saw pieces of Inca pottery and textiles, bits of rope, chunks of wood, even leather and wool sandals. The Inca must have used this spot as a resting-place before attempting to climb to the summit proper. The remains of wooden posts suggest that tentlike structures once stood there. Flat rocks served as flooring, and a layer of grass provided insulation from the cold. Llama feces indicate that the animals had hauled up all this material, which surely weighed no less than two tons.

In the dozens of high-altitude Inca sites I've investigated, I've never seen anything like this system of tented camps and grass-packed trails. There are few building materials on Ampato. Therefore, the Inca had brought wood for tents, stones for floors, blankets for tent coverings, and grass for insulation. They had also built a trail over the more difficult sections of their route to the top of the mountain.

ICY TERRAIN
Anthropologist Johan Reinhard and his team travel through the ice peaks on Nevado Ampato.

DOWN THE MOUNTAIN

Carrying an 80-pound mummy down the mountain to our high camp, 1,500 feet below, proved even more difficult than expected. We were, after all, at an altitude higher than Mount McKinley (the highest mountain peak in North America). We were both weak from having eaten virtually nothing the entire day. The afternoon was drawing on, and it had begun snowing.

We wrapped the mummy in a plastic sheet for protection and tied her to the back of my expedition pack. Dividing the artifacts into plastic bags, we wrapped them in spare clothing.

On the way down I kept slipping on the ash-covered ice and gravel. On the steepest parts of the slope Miguel—who was immediately below me—had to cut steps with his ax. Every time I slipped I managed to prevent disaster by fast footwork or falling backward and using my feet as brakes. Time and again Miguel asked me to

leave the mummy behind. Only later did he explain: "If you'd fallen on me with that load, we'd both have been swept down the mountain."

After dusk our headlamps barely lit the way, and I agreed to leave the mummy for the night. We found a level spot at about 20,000 feet and wedged her safely between two ice pinnacles. Even without the extra weight, it took two hours to reach the high camp. Once we arrived we crawled, exhausted, into our sleeping bags.

"She's all yours," I said to Miguel after I'd finished carrying the mummy down to our high camp the next day. As Miguel struggled to lift the mummy—and realized just what carrying her involved—I couldn't help but smile. The next part of the descent was relatively easy. By 4:30 we'd reached camp, where Henri Wamani, our burro driver, was waiting. We continued down, stopping for the night beside a muddy stream at 15,300 feet.

At dawn we wrapped the mummy in our sleeping pads to insulate her from the warm sun and loaded her onto the burro. "Why are you tying cloth over his eyes?" I asked Henri. "Because he will bolt if he senses he's carrying a dead body." Henri replied solemnly. This sounded reasonable enough. The last thing we needed now was a runaway burro dragging a frozen mummy across the mountainside. Luckily the blindfold worked, and because most of the nonstop 13-hour trek to Cabanaconde held us above 14,000 feet, the temperature inside the sleeping pads stayed around freezing.

Sixty-four hours after we began our descent from the summit of Ampato, the mummy was in a freezer. That evening when I got to Arequipa, I immediately asked José Antonio Chávez, dean of the archaeology department at Catholic University, how much thawing had occurred. "There was still ice on her outer textile when we put her in the freezer," José said, and I felt the tension drain out of me.

A RETURN TRIP

José and I, as co-directors of the High Altitude Sanctuaries of the Southern Andes Project, assembled a full-scale archaeological expedition to return to Ampato. Within a month we were back on the mountain, thanks to speedy issuance of an archaeological permit by Peru's National Institute of Culture and grants from the National Geographic Society.

Fortunately it hadn't snowed. At 19,200 feet the team discovered the remains of two Inca children in sacrificial burials 20 feet apart. The Inca may have chosen this site because it was too difficult to reach the summit. Or possibly the children were less important "companions" to the girl buried on the summit. Both children, one a boy and the other a girl, had been struck by lightning. The Inca believed that the mountain gods used lightning to show their power and even to mark people chosen to become their priests. Villagers still believe this today.

The burials of the children may have taken place during a drought or an eruption of Ampato or Sabancaya. Either event would have killed pastures in the valleys below and polluted or depleted the water supply. This would explain why villagers felt compelled to make sacrificial offerings to appease the mountain gods.

The team tried melting the sides of the tomb with a blowtorch. However, that didn't work because there was so much rock and gravel in the ice. In the end we used water heated in teakettles to melt a channel around the body. This allowed us to free the mummy without soaking her textiles. It took three days of heating, pouring, and picking away. We worked without gloves so we'd be able to feel any textiles mixed in with the water-soaked soil. It was an emotional moment when we at last lifted the body off its flat stone at the bottom of the tomb.

THE MAIDEN'S LAST JOURNEY

It takes an act of the imagination, informed by historical accounts and by our discoveries, to reconstruct the Ampato maiden's last journey. I wonder what the long trek to the summit was like for her. It probably began as a lively procession. Priests most likely led the way. Llamas carried the heavy cargo, which included pottery, food, and ritual offerings. Behind them came the villagers, young and old, singing and dancing as they walked to a "base camp" at 16,300 feet. This consisted of several crude circular and rectangular stone structures and a stone corral for the llamas.

Next day the priests left with the llamas for a campsite at 19,200 feet. Progress in the thin air was slow. By afternoon the girl may have been so weak that she had to be carried. At sunrise the following morning the priests probably made some simple offerings of food and drink to the mountain. The group, llamas included, then

Although she must have been frightened, she may have felt honored to be selected as a sacrifice, imagining perhaps that she was entering a glorious afterlife.

INCA CLOTHING
A gold statue displays
the same style of clothing
as the young woman it
accompanied in death.

MATERIAL GOODS, SPIRITUAL MATTERS
Each of these items played a part in the sacrifice.
Some may have been buried with the children.
1. Llama This wooden llama represents the herds
that the Inca raised. **2. Jar** This decorated ceramic
vessel may have been part of the sacrifice ritual.

3. Plate Ceramic bird-headed plates were found on
Ampato as an offering to the mountain gods.
4. Wooden Cups Many artifacts were found in pairs,
such as these cups. The Inca drank chicha from these
cups during ceremonies.

climbed the 1,200 feet to the grass summit. Here they spent the night.

In the morning more offerings would have been made, and a ritual last meal prepared for the girl. She may have taken a drink of **chicha**. This would have clouded her mind, which at this stage must have been dulled from exhaustion and lack of oxygen. With the ceremonies concluded, they plodded on up the crater ridge to Ampato's summit.

We can only suppose what the girl's last moments were like. Although she must have been frightened, she may have felt honored to be selected as a sacrifice, imagining perhaps that she was entering a glorious afterlife with the gods in a palace within the mountain. If she came from the region, people may have believed she was returning to her ancestral home. They also

may have considered her a direct intermediary between them and the gods. If so, in sacrificing the girl, they could in essence have **deified** her.

I am sometimes questioned about uncovering ancient burial sites. Critics say this shows no respect for the dead. The sad reality, though, is that the looting of such sites by treasure hunters is very likely—even in remote, high places like Ampato. I believe that careful archaeological analysis of sites and permanent protection of their contents in national or academic institutions are both essential and respectful. This belief is shared by the **indigenous** people of the Colca Canyon area, who have expressed their support for our work. The disrespectful alternative—the plunder of our human heritage for profit or for no reason at all—is unacceptable.

UNWRAPPING THE MUMMIES

There aren't many people in the world who are expert at conserving partly frozen mummies. It's by no means as simple as just putting the body in the freezer. Sonia Guillén of the Mallqui Center in Ilo, who is an expert on mummies dried out by the sun, says the Ampato maiden is special. "Juanita is such a challenge because there are no set rules as to how to work with a frozen body with 500-year-old textiles on it."

She sought advice from specialists abroad. One expert, Horst Seidler from the Institute of Human Biology at the University of Vienna, Austria, urged removing the textiles immediately to protect both the clothing and the body, "First, second, and third, you must remove the textiles."

To avoid thawing the mummy, we initially limited her time outside the freezer to about 30 minutes a day. José Antonio Chávez later decided to use ice packs to keep the body frozen. The sessions were longer but no less tense. The thought of an irreversible error—damaging the girl's skin or a textile—haunted the team.

When we uncovered the girl's right hand and saw that she was clutching her *aksu*, or body wrap, in a death grip, her humanity really hit us. We now have to figure out how to remove the textile without damaging the skin of her hand.

At this point the mummy is only partly unwrapped, yet William Conklin has reconstructed exactly how the girl was clothed. He has also observed that her textiles are strikingly similar to those on the female statues buried with her. The statues may have represented goddesses. This young woman, who could have been deified through her sacrificial death, was dressed in a manner befitting her place in the spirit world.

Taken as a whole, the Ampato discoveries promise many new insights about the Inca way of life. In their early death, the Ampato maiden and the two other Inca sacrifices have given new life to the memory of their people—one of ancient history's greatest civilizations.

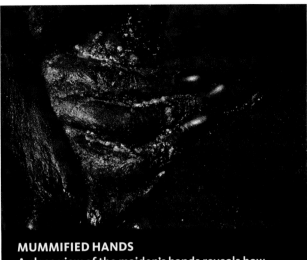

MUMMIFIED HANDS
A close view of the maiden's hands reveals how she clutched her clothing to try to stay warm.

Postscript: In 1999, Johan Reinhard co-directed an expedition that led to the discovery of three more Inca mummies. These mummies are far better preserved than the ice maiden found in 1995. DNA analysis of the mummies has helped archaeologists determine if they are related, and analysis of isotopes, variants of atoms of the same element, has identified their diet.

THINK ABOUT IT! ||||||||||||||||||||||||||

1 **Make Inferences** Why do you think the people of the Colca Canyon area support the work of Johan Reinhard and his colleagues?

2 **Make Generalizations** What are the advantages and disadvantages of working at high-altitude archaeological sites?

BACKGROUND & VOCABULARY

chicha (CHEE-chah) *n.* a drink of South America made from corn

deify *v.* (DEE-uh-fy) to make an object of worship like a god

indigenous *adj.* (IHN-dihj-ih-nuhs) living or occurring naturally in a particular area

spondylus shell (SPAHN-duh-lihs shehl) *n.* a type of shell used in ceremonies by people in the Andes Mountains

The effort to preserve Peru's cultural artifacts has many champions. One is archaeologist Luis Jaime Castillo Butters, a Vice-Minister in the Ministry of Culture of Peru and a teacher at the Pontificia Universidad Católica del Perú. Professor Castillo directs the San José de Moro Archaeological Project, one of Peru's largest research projects. He's on the front lines for uncovering amazing treasures and deploying them to help the Peruvian people.

DOCUMENT 1 Primary Source
Making a Difference

Luis Jaime, as he is informally called, credits his family and his teachers for inspiring him to become an archaeologist. For him, archaeology fulfills both a personal and communal purpose.

All my interests [combined] . . . in the pursuit of answers to big questions about the past and the present. . . . Archaeology has a bit of everything: half sciences and half humanities, fieldwork and lab, computers and drawing boards. . . . I think that everyone has to find a niche where they can make a difference, and doing seriously what we do makes a difference, transforms lives, makes the world a better place. . . . In my country the past has become very much part of the present. It is front-page news and has made people proud and bettered their lives.

from "Explorers Bio," nationalgeographic.com/explorers/bios/luis-jaime-castillo/

CONSTRUCTED RESPONSE

1. According to Luis Jaime, what drew him to becoming an archaeologist?

DOCUMENT 2 Primary Source
Preserving Community

Working on a dig can be a tough job. But shouldering heavy tools, putting in long hours, and getting down in the dirt is the easy part. Working among the local people—often descendants of those whose artifacts are being unearthed—archaeologists see firsthand the sometimes difficult conditions these families endure every day. In this passage, Luis Jaime reflects on what can be done to improve their lives and the shared responsibility to help.

The most challenging experience in the field has been working with the community in San José de Moro and learning about the real world with them. We work under the Sustainable Preservation Initiative . . . where to preserve the site we have to change the lives of the local people and create opportunities for their development. . . . A lot of my time is devoted to this end, to foster artisans that produce the best replicas of Moche ceramics in the world, to train young kids in the crafts that will support their families, and to organize the community and help them in their needs. But it is not an easy thing to do.

from "Explorers Bio," nationalgeographic.com/explorers/bios/luis-jaime-castillo/

CONSTRUCTED RESPONSE

2. Based on the comments by Luis Jaime, what personal traits do you think archaeologists should have to handle their work?

What are the challenges and rewards of working as an **archaeologist**?

BANCO CENTRAL DE RESERVA DEL PERÚ, Lima, Peru.

DOCUMENT 3 Secondary Source
Drone Technology

Excavating at Incahuasi in early 2014, Luis Jaime pioneered the use of a new technology in archaeology—unmanned aircraft, or drones. This 21st-century method of gathering photos and more precise data promises to change the way archaeologists do their jobs. More importantly, drones are proving effective in the fight against the looting of archaeological sites for personal profit. Looting often leaves behind ruined landscapes and communities. Drones are one way archaeologists are addressing the problem.

CONSTRUCTED RESPONSE
3. How might the use of drones make the work of archaeologists easier and more accurate?

Luis Jaime operates an archaeological drone at Cerro Cheoeon, Peru.

PUT IT TOGETHER |||||||||||||||||||||||||||||||||||||||||||||||||||||||||||||||||||||||||||||||||||||||||||||||||||||||||||||||||

Review Think about your responses to the Constructed Response questions and what you can infer from the articles and Luis Jaime about the rewards and challenges of archaeology.

Summarize Create a two-column chart with the headings "Rewards" and "Challenges." Write down your ideas about the parts of their work that archaeologists might find rewarding or challenging.

Write Write a topic sentence that answers this question: What are the challenges and rewards of working as an archaeologist? Then write a paragraph that supports your topic sentence using evidence from the documents.

INDEX

||||||||||||||||||||||||||||||||||||||||||||||||||||||

SKILLS